Knitwear
by Sasha Kagan

Knitwear
by Sasha Kagan

GUILD OF
MASTER CRAFTSMAN
PUBLICATIONS

First published 2008 by
Guild of Master Craftsman Publications Ltd
Castle Place, 166 High Street
Lewes, East Sussex BN7 1XU

ISBN-13: 978-1-86108-519-1
ISBN-10: 1-86108-519-2

Production Manager: Jim Bulley
Managing Editor: Gerrie Purcell
Project Editor: Gill Parris
Managing Art Editor: Gilda Pacitti
Designer: James Hollywell

Photographer: Chris Gloag
Illustrator: Simon Rodway

Set in Avenir and Linoscript
Colour origination by Altaimage
Printed and bound by Colourprint offset in China

A NOTE ON MEASUREMENTS

Although care has been taken to ensure that metric measurements are true and accurate, they are only conversions from imperial; they have been rounded up or down to the nearest convenient equivalent in cases where the imperial measurements themselves are only approximate. When following the projects, use either imperial or metric measurements. Do not mix units.

Foreword

I discovered the work of Sasha Kagan about 20 years ago. By happenstance I came across her first book, *The Sasha Kagan Sweater Book*, and was mesmerized by her wonderful design sense and her unique approach to knitting. I remember thinking that I had made a wonderful discovery!

I have always admired the way Sasha takes inspiration from her surroundings, and throughout this book you will see the influence of the beautiful Welsh countryside she calls home.

Sasha has an innate ability to combine motifs and textures and to use colour creatively – when I think of her work, the images that come to mind are beautifully toned falling leaves, pretty wildflowers scattered against a lace or cabled background, delicate design details like miniature ruffles, and ties, or contrasting bands of color. All the while, Sasha is able to maintain a balance in her designs, making each piece pleasing to the discerning eye, as well as ultimately flattering to the figure.

As Editor-in-Chief of *Vogue Knitting* Magazine, I have had the pleasure of working with Sasha professionally for many years now, as well as getting to know her personally. We have collaborated on some really lovely projects, including some you will see featured in these pages.

This beautiful book is a retrospective of a life dedicated to designing beautiful knits. You are about to be treated to 22 of her personal favourite knitting works. The canvases she uses are her Sweaters, Cardigans, Coats, Jackets, and Wraps and Scarves, all delightfully patterned and coloured in her signature artistic style.

Trisha Malcolm
Editorial Director
Vogue Knitting Magazine

Contents

Introduction

KNITTING FOR PLEASURE and recreation is, and always has been, a fantastically rewarding pastime. It is wonderful to see the resurgence of interest and enthusiasm for the craft in today's world of knitting clubs, exhibitions, festivals, workshops, getaways, knit-ins, blogs, Internet interactions and worldwide seminars. Knitting is no longer regarded as a fuddy-duddy granny pursuit but a hip and happening hobby for all to enjoy.

In the seven years since I wrote *Country Inspiration* – my collection of patterns for knitters who love designs inspired by nature – I have seen new knitting magazines hit the news-stands, and yarn shops open instead of close. But, most importantly, I see a new generation of young knitters taking up their needles and enjoying the satisfaction of making their own creations.

Knitting is such a versatile medium of expression. My personal passion has always been colour, texture and the use of repeating patterns to make fabric for classic knits. This collection of 22 designs continues that theme. The designs were originally commissioned by *Knitting* magazine, *Rowan*, *Vogue* and *Woman's Weekly*. Some have evolved from the originals with the introduction of new colourways, change of length to a jacket, reworking of patterns with new yarns and general fine-tuning. I have begun to use lace to make fabrics more airy, cables as contrast to motifs and crochet for a subtle addition of accent colour.

Yarn is of utmost importance in any knitting project and I advise you to go for the best quality available, both for your knitting experience and the pleasure of wearing your finished pieces. My favourites are Rowan and Jaeger, companies which are constantly developing new fibre blends, tweeds and silks to tempt the knitter into ever more sensuous knitting experiences.

I also like to support the 'shop local' ethos – not only does it save CO_2 emissions from aeroplanes carrying yarn around the globe, but also supports our UK fleece-producing farmers. Jamieson and Smith in the remote Shetland Islands have a wonderful range of 4-ply Shetland colours which are ideal for my country-inspired pieces, such as Heartsease (see page 106), while UK Alpaca, in Devon, have developed an Alpaca/Blue-faced Leicester yarn with a fabulous drape, wonderful for giving movement to a garment; this yarn was used for Suzani (page 130) and Poppy (page 76).

Exciting yarn is also being produced in the USA: Brown Sheep Company's Cotton Fine, a blend of 80% cotton/20% merino wool, was *Vogue Knitting* magazine's choice for Liberty Floral (page 108) and Dale of Norway's Dalegarn Tiur, a mixture of 60% mohair/40% wool their choice for my Hebron Stripe (page 66). If you can't find the yarn in your local wool shop you will see all the necessary information for ordering listed in Resources (page154). If you decide to substitute yarns, please remember to knit up a swatch first, to make sure you are getting the correct tension (gauge). If the swatch is too large, go down a needle size, if too small go up a needle size.

The Techniques chapter on pages 142 to 153 will help you with all aspects of knitting used in my designs. If you are daunted by the intarsia technique take a look at my detailed explanations of the different methods of knitting with colour. Diagrams show the techniques and close-up photos of both the front and the back of the fabric illustrate how the technique is achieved. Choose a chart and have a practice, its really not that difficult and, if you have only knitted in one colour before, a whole new world will open up for you. My colours are there to guide you but do feel free to make up your own colour combinations and have as much fun as I do playing with colour.

As I live in an isolated area of Wales contact with my fellow knitters and fibre fanatics happens at workshops, festivals, shows and lecture tours; the enthusiasm for the fibre arts is very contagious at these events and I do urge you to get out and about if you can and take part in the new knitting revolution. Information on fibre-related events can be found in knitting magazines, the websites of yarn companies, designers and knitting organizations.

I hope you will enjoy my latest collection of knitwear designs. My well-known signature knitting kits are available for all designs in the book. For details, contact me at the address on page 156. I am always happy to receive feedback from my fans, so please also feel free to write or e-mail me with your knitting experiences.

Happy Knitting!

Diagonal Flowers
Pattern page 62

Nautical
Pattern page 64

Hebron Stripe

Pattern page 66

Flower Power
Pattern page 68

Valentine
Pattern page 72

Rosebud

Pattern page 80

Pebble

Pattern page 84

Tiny Flower
Pattern page 88

Snowberry
Pattern page 92

Heath

Pattern page 98

Aster

Pattern page 102

Heartsease

Pattern page 106

Liberty Floral
Pattern page 108

KNITWEAR BY SASHA KAGAN

Cable Flower

Pattern page 112

Harlequin
Pattern page 116

Caliope
Pattern page 122

Baluchistan Stripe
Pattern page 126

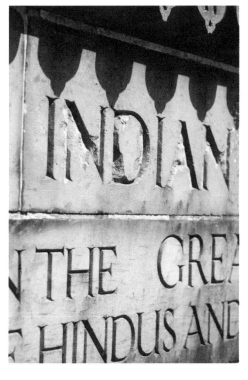

Suzani
Pattern page 130

Columbine

Pattern page 134

Laurel

Pattern page 136

CHAPTER ONE

Sweaters

Main image page 10

Diagonal Flowers

A 1940s-inspired sweater with wide diagonal ribs. A timeless cotton piece for a classic summer wardrobe.

SIZES
To fit bust 32[34:36:38:40]in
(81[86:91:97:102]cm)
See schematic for actual measurements

MATERIALS
Rowan 4-ply cotton 186yd (170m)
per 50g ball
8(8:9:9:9) balls colour A:
    Navy (150)
1(1:1:1:1) ball colour B:
    Bluebell (136)
1(1:1:1:1) ball colour C:
    Honeydew (140)
1(1:1:1:1) ball colour D:
    Fennel (135)
1(1:1:1:1) ball colour E:
    Violetta (146)
1(1:1:1:1) ball colour F:
    Orchid (120)
1(1:1:1:1) ball colour G:
    Bloom (132)
Needles: 1 pair each 2.25mm (US 1)
and 3mm (US 2/3)
Stitch holder

TENSION
28 sts and 38 rows = 4in (10cm)
measured over st st pattern using
larger needles.

STITCHES USED
Stocking stitch (page 144)
Garter stitch (page 144)

Front
Using smaller needles and colour A
cast on 117[123:131:137:145] sts.
Work in garter st for 4 rows, ending
with a WS row.
Change to larger needles.
Using the **woven intarsia** technique
(described on page 148), starting
and ending rows as indicated and
repeating the 44 row patt repeat,
cont in patt from chart as folls:
Inc 1 st at each end of 15th and
every foll 14th row until there are
129[135:143:149:157) sts.
Cont straight until chart row
22[24:20:22:18] has been worked for
the 3rd time, ending with a WS row.
Shape armholes
Keeping chart correct, cast off
4[5:5:6:6] sts at beg of next 2 rows.
121[125:133:137:145] sts.
Dec 1 st at each end of next
5[5:7:7:9] rows, then on foll 5[6:6:7:7]
alt rows.
101[103:107:109:113] sts.**
Work a further 7[3:5:1:3] rows, ending
after chart row 2 and with a WS row.
Divide for neck
Next row (RS): Patt 50[51:53:54:56]
sts and turn, leaving rem sts on
a holder.
Work each side of neck separately.
Work 1 row.
Dec 1 st at neck edge of next and
every foll alt row until 25[25:27:27:29]
sts rem.
Work 1 row, ending with a WS row.
Shape shoulder
Cast off 8[8:9:9:9] sts at beg and dec
1 st at end of next row.
16[16:17:17:19] sts.
Work 1 row.
Cast off 8[8:9:9:9] sts at beg of
next row.
Work 1 row.
Cast off rem 8[8:8:8:10] sts.
With RS facing, rejoin yarns to rem
sts, p2tog, patt to end.
Complete to match first side,
reversing shapings.

Back
Work as given for front to **.
Cont straight until back matches front
to start of shoulder shaping, ending
with a WS row.

Shape shoulders and back neck
Cast off 8[8:9:9:9] sts at beg of next
2 rows.
85[87:89:91:95] sts.
Next row (RS): Cast off 8[8:9:9:9] sts,
patt until there are 12[12:12:12:14]
sts on right needle and turn, leaving
rem sts on a holder.
Work each side of neck separately.
Cast off 4 sts at beg of next row.
Cast off rem 8[8:8:8:10] sts.
With RS facing, rejoin yarns to rem
sts, cast off centre 45[47:47:49:49]
sts, patt to end.
Complete to match first side,
reversing shapings.

Sleeves
Using smaller needles and colour A
cast on 59[59:61:63:63] sts.
Work in garter st for 4 rows, ending
with a WS row.
Change to larger needles.
Starting and ending rows as indicated,
taking inc sts into pattern, cont
in patt from chart, shaping sides
by inc 1 st at each end of
7th[7th:7th:7th:5th] and every
foll 8th[8th:8th:8th:6th] row to
81[91:99:101:79] sts, then on every
foll 10th[10th:0:0:8th] row – first,
second and fifth sizes only – until
there are 93[95:99:101:105] sts.
Cont straight until sleeve measures
17¾[17¾:18:18:18]in
(45[45:46:46:46]cm), ending with a
WS row.
Shape top
Keeping chart correct, cast off
4[5:5:6:6] sts at beg of next 2 rows.
85[85:89:89:93] sts.
Dec 1 st at each end next 3 rows, 2
foll alt rows, then on every foll 4th
row until 59[59:63:63:67] sts.
Work 1 row, ending with a WS row.
Dec 1 st at each end of next and
every foll alt row until 49 sts rem,
then on foll 3 rows, ending with a WS
row. Cast off rem 43 sts.

Finishing
Tidy loose ends back into their own
colours. Block pieces to correct
measurements.
Join right shoulder seam.

Neckband

Using smaller needles and colour A and with RS facing pick up and knit 44[46:46:48:48] sts down left side of neck, place marker on needle, pick up and knit 44[46:46:48:48] sts up right side of neck, then 53[55:55:57:57] sts from back. 141[147:147:153:153] sts.

Row 1 (WS): Knit to within 2 sts of marker, k2tog, k2tog tbl, knit to end.

Row 2: As row 1.

Cast off k-wise (on WS), decreasing either side of marker as before. Join L shoulder seam. Set in sleeves. Join side seams and sleeve seams. Steam seams.

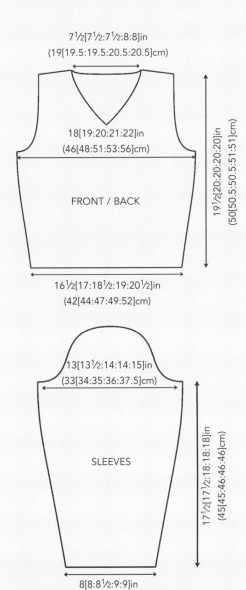

7½[7½:7½:8:8]in
(19[19.5:19.5:20.5:20.5]cm)

18[19:20:21:22]in
(46[48:51:53:56]cm)

FRONT / BACK

19½[20:20:20:20]in
(50[50.5:50.5:51:51]cm)

16½[17:18½:19:20½]in
(42[44:47:49:52]cm)

13[13½:14:14:15]in
(33[34:35:36:37.5]cm)

SLEEVES

17½[17½:18:18:18]in
(45[45:46:46:46]cm)

8[8:8½:9:9]in
(21[21:22:22.5:22.5]cm)

44 row patt rep

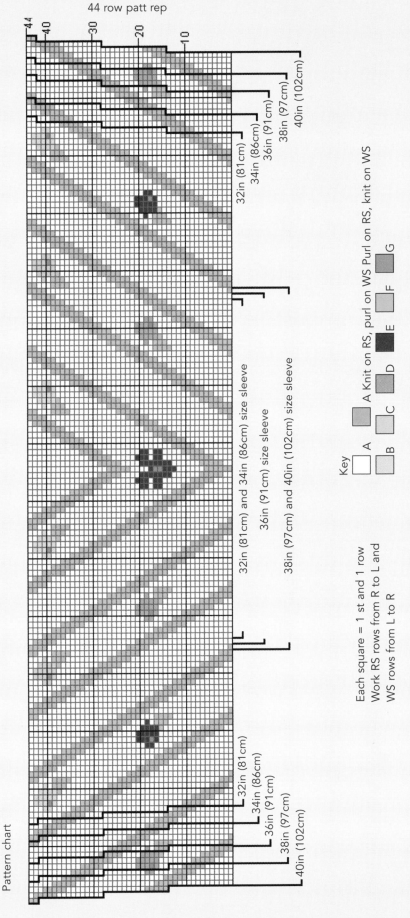

32in (81cm)
34in (86cm)
36in (91cm)
38in (97cm)
40in (102cm)

32in (81cm) and 34in (86cm) size sleeve
36in (91cm) size sleeve
38in (97cm) and 40in (102cm) size sleeve

32in (81cm)
34in (86cm)
36in (91cm)
38in (97cm)
40in (102cm)

Pattern chart

Key

A — A Knit on RS, purl on WS
B
C
D
E — Purl on RS, knit on WS
F
G

Each square = 1 st and 1 row
Work RS rows from R to L and
WS rows from L to R

Main image page 13

Nautical

This classic crew-neck sailing sweater sports intarsia boat motifs and giant cables. A must for sunny seaside outings and nautical expeditions.

SIZES
To fit bust 32[37:40]in (81[94:101]cm)
See schematic for actual measurements

MATERIALS
Rowan Cashsoft DK
142yd (130m) per 50g ball
8(9:11) balls colour A:
    Ballad Blue (508)
1(1:1) ball colour B:
    Cream (500)
1(1:1) ball colour C:
    Poppy (512)
1(1:1) ball colour D:
    Navy (514)
Needles: 1 pair each 3mm (US 3)
and 4mm (US 6)
Stitch holders

TENSION
26 sts and 32 rows = 4in (10cm)
measured using 4mm needles over
patt unstretched using larger needles.

STITCHES USED
Stocking stitch (page 144)
Moss (seed) stitch (page 144)
Cable 8 Front (C8F, page 145)
Cable 8 Back (C8B, page 145)

TIPS
Versatility in sizing is achieved because the fabric is naturally quite stretchy width-wise. Measurements are for the totally relaxed garment. When measuring lengths during knitting, smooth out on a flat surface to give measurement width(s) in diagram before measuring length.

Back
Using smaller needles and colour A cast on 108[124:138] sts. Work in moss st for 1in (2.5cm).
Change to larger needles and, using the **woven intarsia** technique (described on page 148), place intarsia pattern thus: Work 6[14:5] sts in st st, rep chart from st 1 to st 32 3[3:4] times, work 6[14:5] sts in st st.
Rep chart from bottom to top until piece measures 11½in (29.5cm) from beg.
Shape armholes
Cast off 4[6:7] sts at beg of next 2 rows. Dec 1 st at each end of next 3[3:4] rows then on foll 2[4:5] alt rows, then on every foll 4th row until 86[92:98] sts rem. Work straight until armhole measures 8[8½:9½]in (20[22:24]cm) ending with RS facing for next row.
Shape shoulders and back neck
Cast off 6[7:8] sts at beg of next 2 rows.
Next row: (RS) Cast off 6[7:8] sts, patt until there are 10[11:12] sts on R needle and turn, leaving rem sts on a holder and work each side of neck separately.
Cast off 4 sts at beg of next row. Cast off rem 6[7:8] sts.
With RS facing, rejoin yarns to rem sts. Cast off centre 42 sts, work to end. Cast off 6[7:8] sts at beg of next row. Cast off 4 sts at beg of next row, work to end. Cast off rem 6[7:8] sts.

Front
Work as for back until 20 rows less have been worked than on back to beg of shoulder shaping ending with RS facing for next row.
Shape neck
Next row: (RS) Work 31[34:37] sts and turn, leaving rem sts on a holder. Work each side of neck separately.

Cast off 4 sts at neck edge on next row, work 1 row. Dec 1 st at neck edge on next 5 rows, work 1 row. Dec 1 st at neck edge on next and every foll alt row until 18[21:24] sts rem. Work 1 row, ending at shoulder edge.
Shape shoulder
Cast off 6[7:8] sts at beg of next and foll alt row. Work 1 row. Cast off rem 6[7:8] sts.
With RS facing, rejoin yarn to rem sts. Cast off centre 24 sts. Work to end. Complete to match first side, reversing shapings.

Sleeves
Using smaller needles and colour A cast on 60[64:68] sts. Work in moss st until work measures 3½in (9cm). Change to larger needles and foll chart, noting starting beg and end of patt and taking extra sts into patt as they occur and at the same time, inc 1 st at each end of next and every foll 10[10:8]th row to 68[74:78] sts, then on every foll 12[10:10]th row until there are 72[80:88] sts. Work straight until sleeve measures 16.5[17:17½]in (42[43:44]cm).
Shape top
Cast off 4 sts at beg of next 2 rows. Dec 1 st at each end foll 16[17:17] alt rows, then on every foll 3rd row until 24[26:28] sts rem. Cast off.

Finishing
Tidy loose ends back into their own colours. Steam gently to correct (unstretched) measurements.
Join R shoulder seam.
Neckband
With RS facing, using smaller needles and colour A, pick up and k15 sts down L side of neck, 24 sts from front neck, 15 sts up R side of neck then 50 sts from back neck (104 sts). Work in moss st for 1in (2.5cm), cast off. Join L shoulder seam. Set in sleeves. Join side and sleeve seams. Steam seams.

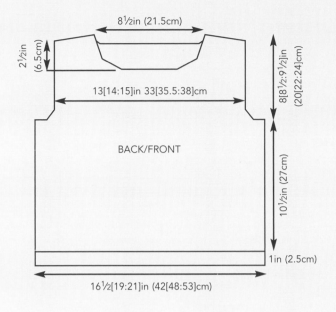

8½in (21.5cm)

2½in (6.5cm)

13[14:15]in 33[35.5:38]cm

8[8½:9½]in (20[22:24]cm)

BACK/FRONT

10½in (27cm)

1in (2.5cm)

16½[19:21]in (42[48:53]cm)

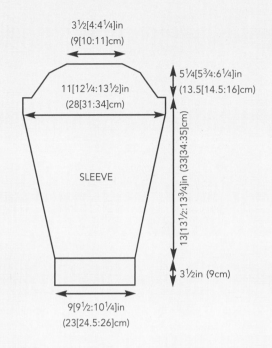

3½[4:4¼]in (9[10:11]cm)

11[12¼:13½]in (28[31:34]cm)

5¼[5¾:6¼]in (13.5[14.5:16]cm)

SLEEVE

13[13½:13¾]in (33[34:35]cm)

3½in (9cm)

9[9½:10¼]in (23[24.5:26]cm)

Pattern chart

32 sts x 32 rows

1 square = 1 st and 1 row
Read RS rows from R to L
WS rows from L to R

Key

A

B

C

D

purl on RS
knit on ws

Work cable twist to L

Work cable twist to R

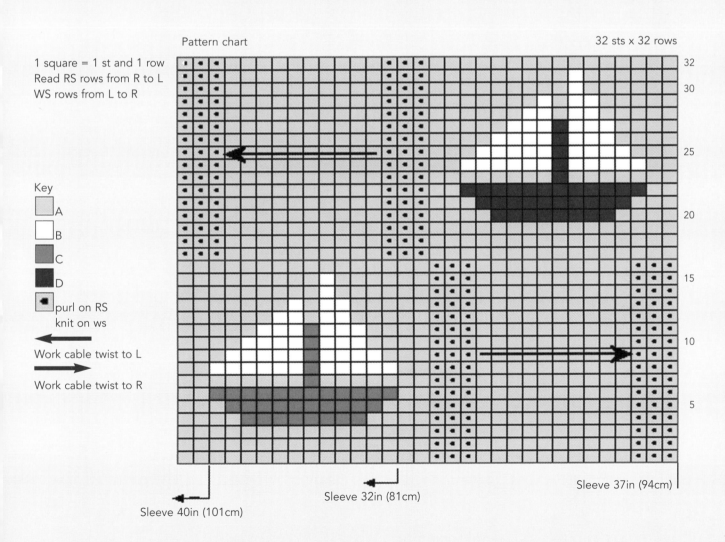

Sleeve 40in (101cm)

Sleeve 32in (81cm)

Sleeve 37in (94cm)

Main image page 14

Hebron Stripe

Embroidery from the Far East was the inspiration for this fitted evening sweater. The wide neck is balanced by long sleeves and an optional ribbon under the bust.

SIZES
To fit bust 32[35:38]in (81[89:98]cm)
See schematic for actual measurements

MATERIALS
Dale of Norway TIUR
126yds (115m) per 50g ball
8(9:10) balls main colour (MC):
  Black (0090)
1(1:1) ball colour A:
  Orange (3436)
1(1:1) ball colour B:
  Red (4027)
1(1:1) ball colour C:
  Olive (9853)
1(1:1) ball colour D:
  Magenta (4545)
1(1:1) ball colour E:
  Pink (4425)
Needles: 1 pair each 2.75mm (US 2) and 3.5mm (US 4)
Ribbon: 59in (150cm) long and 1in (2.5cm) wide

TENSION
30 sts and 31 rows = 4in (10cm) measured over st st and chart pattern using larger needles; 50 sts = 4in (10cm) over twisted rib using smaller needles.

STITCHES USED
1 x 1 twisted rib (page 144)
Stocking stitch (page 144)
2-colour stranded knitting (page 147)

Back
With smaller needles and MC, cast on 120[132:144] sts. Work in twisted rib for 8in (20.5cm), end with a WS row. Change to larger needles.
Beg chart
Beg with st 1 and, using the **woven intarsia** technique (described on page 148), work sts 1–40 3 times, work sts 0[1–12:1–24] once more. Cont as established, working rows 1–54 until piece measures 12in (30.5cm) from beg, end with a WS row.
Armhole shaping
Cont to work chart, cast off 7 sts at beg of next 2 rows, dec 1 st each side every other row 6[8:10] times, then every 4th row 2 times more – 90[98:106] sts. Work even until armhole measures 5[5½:6]in (12.5[14:15]cm), end with a WS row.
Neck shaping
Next row: (RS) Cont to work chart, work 35[39:43] sts, join a 2nd ball of yarn and cast off centre 20 sts, work to end. Working both sides at once, dec 1 st at each neck edge every row 20 times. Work even until armhole measures 8[8½:9]in (20.5[21.5:23]cm). Cast off rem 15[19:23] sts each side for shoulders.

Front
Work as for back until piece measures 16[16½:17]in (40.5[42:43]cm) from beg, end with a WS row.
Neck shaping
Work 30[34:38] sts, join a 2nd ball of yarn and cast off centre 30 sts, work to end. Working both sides at once, dec 1 st at each neck edge every other row 15 times. Continue straight until piece measures same as back to shoulders. Cast off rem 15[19:23] sts each side for shoulders.

Sleeves
With smaller needles and MC, cast on 94 sts. Work in twisted rib as foll: K2tbl, *p2, k2tbl; rep from * to end.

K the knit sts tbl and p the purl sts for 11in (28cm), inc 0(4:8) sts evenly across last WS row – 94[98:102] sts. Change to larger needles.
Beg chart
Beg with row 25, work sts 1–40 twice, work sts 1–14[1–18:1–22]. Cont as established, work through chart row 50, then work rows 1–54 until piece measures 18in (45.5cm), end with same row as back to armhole shaping.
Shape top
Cont in chart, cast off 7 sts at beg of next 2 rows, dec 1 st each side of every row 5 times, every other row 2[4:6] times, every 4th row 6 times, every other row 6 times, every row 7 times – cast off rem 28 sts.

Finishing
Tidy loose ends back into their own colours. Block pieces to correct measurements, do not block ribs. Sew one shoulder seam.
Neckband
With RS facing, smaller needles and MC, pick up and k144 sts evenly around neck edge. Work in twisted rib for 4 rows. Cast off in rib. Sew 2nd shoulder and neckband seam. Set in sleeves. Sew side and sleeve seams. Steam seams.
Side loops (make 2)
With smaller needles and MC, cast on 12 sts. Cast off. Attach loops at top of rib on side seams. Thread ribbon through loops and tie in bow at centre front.

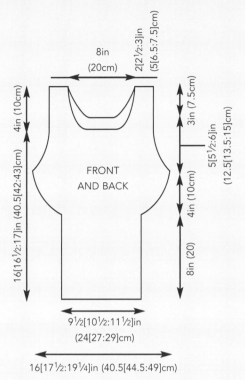

8in
(20cm)

2[2½:3]in
(5[6.5:7.5]cm)

4in (10cm)

FRONT
AND BACK

16[16½:17]in (40.5[42:43]cm)

3in (7.5cm)

5[5½:6]in
(12.5[13.5:15]cm)

4in (10cm)

8in (20)

9½[10½:11½]in
(24[27:29]cm)

16[17½:19¼]in (40.5[44.5:49]cm)

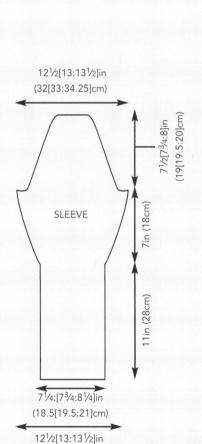

12½[13:13½]in
(32[33:34.25]cm)

7½[7¾:8]in
(19[19.5:20]cm)

7in (18cm)

SLEEVE

11in (28cm)

7¼:[7¾:8¼]in
(18.5[19.5:21]cm)

12½[13:13½]in
(32[33:34.25]cm)

Pattern chart

40 sts x 54 rows

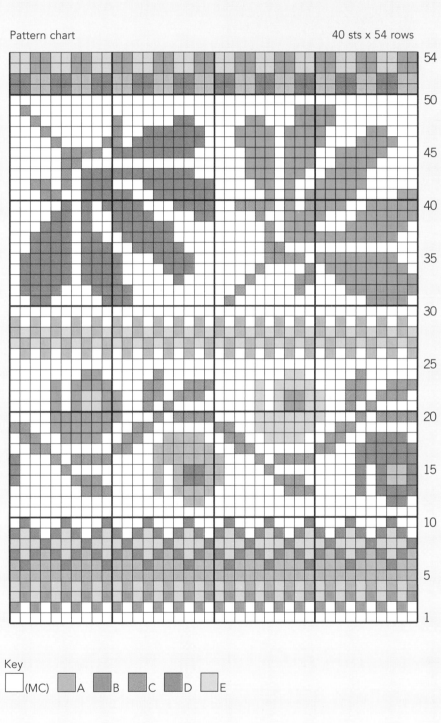

Key

☐ (MC) ☐ A ☐ B ☐ C ☐ D ☐ E

1 square = 1 st and 1 row. Read
RS rows from R to L and WS
rows from L to R

Main image page 17

Flower Power

A 1960s-inspired design is brought up to date with fitted body, turtleneck collar and long ribbed sleeves. A dramatic piece for cooler days.

SIZES

To fit bust 32[34:38]in (81[86:91]cm)
See schematic for actual measurements

MATERIALS

Rowan RYC cashsoft DK 130m (142yd) per 50g ball
12[13:14] balls colour A:
    Poppy (512)
1[1:1] ball colour B:
    Black (519)
Rowan wool/cotton 113m (123yd) per 50g ball
1[1:1] ball colour C:
    Flower (943)
1[1:1] ball colour D:
    Clear (941)
1[1:1] ball colour E:
    Hiss (952)
Rowan Kid Classic 140m (153yd) per 50g ball
1[1:1] ball colour F:
    Crushed Velvet (825)
1[1:1] ball colour G:
    Royal (835)
Needles: 1 pair each 4mm (US 6), 3.75mm (US 5) and 3.25mm (US 4)
Stitch holders

TENSION

22 sts and 29 rows = 4in (10cm) measured over st st and chart pattern using larger needles.

STITCHES USED

Stocking stitch (page 144)
2 x 2 twisted rib (page 144)

Back

With smaller needles and colour A cast on 90[102:114] sts.
1st twisted rib row: (K1b) twice, * p2, (k1b) twice, repeat from * to end.
2nd twisted rib row: (P1b) twice, * K2, (p1b) twice repeat from * to end.
Repeat last 2 rows, 19 times more. Change to larger needles.
Row 1: Knit in colour A
Row 2: Purl in colour A
Row 3: K 0[0:12] edge sts of 3rd row of chart, (knit across 30 sts pattern repeat and, using the **woven intarsia** technique described on page 148) 3 times, k0[12:12] edge sts.
Row 4: Purl 0[12:12] edge sts of 4th row of chart, (purl across 30 sts pattern repeat) 3 times, p0[0:12] edge sts keeping continuity of chart as placed, work another 28 rows. These 32 rows form pattern. Pattern another 32 rows.

Shape armholes

Keeping pattern correct, cast off 3 sts at beginning of next 2 rows, then dec 1 st each end of next row and 2 following alternate rows, 78[90:102] sts. **
Pattern another 47[51:55] rows.

Shape shoulders

Cast off 12[18:12] sts at beginning of next 2[2:4] rows. Leave remaining 54 sts on a stitch holder.

Front

Work as back to **.
Pattern another 25[29:33] rows.

Shape neck

Next row: Pattern 24[30:36], turn and work on these sts for left front neck.

Left front neck

*** Cast off 3 sts at beginning of next row, then dec 1 st at neck edge on next 5 rows and 4 following alternate rows, 12[18:24] sts.
Pattern another 7 rows.

Shape shoulder

Cast off 12[18:12] sts at beginning of next row and 0[0:1] following alternate row. ***

Right front neck

With RS facing, slip centre 30 sts on st holder, rejoin yarn to remaining sts and pattern to end, 24[30:36] sts.
Pattern 1 row.
Work as left front neck from *** to ***.

Sleeves

With smaller needles and colour A, cast on 72[76:80] sts.
1st twisted rib row: K1b, p2, * (k1b) twice, p2, repeat from * to last st, k1b.
2nd twisted rib row: P1b, K2, * (p1b) twice, k2, repeat from * to last st, p1b.
Repeat last 2 rows, 31 times more, inc 0[8:4] sts evenly across last row, 72[84:84] sts.
Change to larger needles.
Working edge sts as given on back for 3rd size and 30 sts pattern repeat twice, continue until 84 rows of pattern have been worked.

Shape top

Keeping pattern correct, cast off 3 sts at beginning of next 4 rows, then dec 1 st at beginning of next 34[28:32] rows, 26[44:40] sts.
Dec 1 st each end of next 0[8:6] rows, then cast off 3 sts at beginning of next 2 rows.
Cast off remaining 20[22:22] sts.

Turtleneck Collar

Join right shoulder seam.
With RSF using smaller needles and colour A, pick up and k24 sts down left front neck, k30 sts from centre front, pick up and k24 sts up right front neck, then k54 sts from back neck, 132 sts.
1st twisted rib row: P1b, k2, * (p1b) twice, k2, repeat from * to last st, p1b.
2nd twisted rib row: K1b, p2, * (k1b) twice, p2, repeat from * to last st, k1b.
Repeat the last 2 rows, 22 times more, then work the first row again.
Change to larger needles.
Next row: K1, (p1b) twice, * k2, (p1b) twice, repeat from * to last st, k1.
Next row: P1, (k1b) twice, * p2, (k1b) twice, repeat from * to last st, p1.
Repeat last 2 rows, 20 times more.
Cast off loosely in rib.

Finishing

Tidy loose ends back into their own colours. Block pieces to correct measurements. Do not block ribs. Join left shoulder seam and turtleneck collar, reversing seam on collar to allow for fold back. Set sleeves into armholes. Join side and sleeve seams. Steam seams.

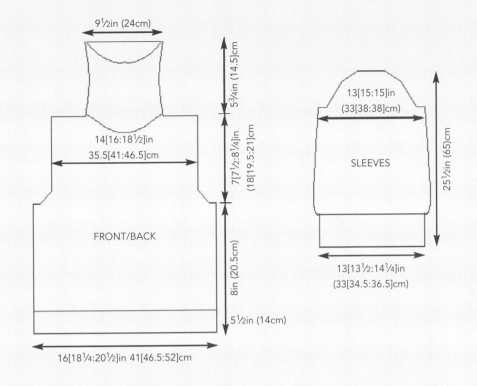

Pattern chart   30 sts x 32 rows

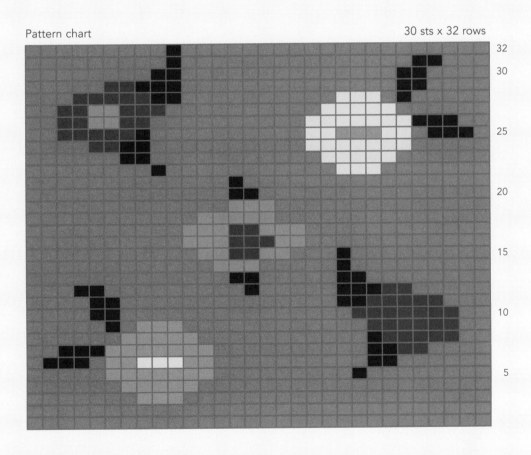

1 square = 1 st and 1 row. Read RS rows from R to L and WS rows from L to R

Key

CHAPTER TWO

Cardigans

Main image page 18

Valentine

Love is in the air with this light-hearted cardigan, and the two-colour heart motifs make it an easy piece to knit.

SIZES
To fit bust 36[38:40]in (91[96:102]cm)
See schematic for actual measurements

MATERIALS
Rowan Kid Classic
153yd (140m) per 50g ball
7[8:9] balls colour A:
    Feather (828)
2[2:3] balls colour B:
    Cherry Red (847)
Needles: 1 pair each of 3.75mm
(US 5) and 4.5mm (US 7)
Buttons: 6 x ¾in (2cm)
Stitch holder

TENSION
20 sts and 28 rows = 4in (10cm) over intarsia and stocking stitch pattern using larger needles.

STITCHES USED
Stocking stitch (page 144)
Bobble rib (see right)
2 x 2 rib (page 144)
Woven and linked intarsia (page 148)

KNITTING NOTES
If desired (A) can be carried across small hearts (intarsia woven method), but should not be carried across back of large hearts (intarsia linked method).

Bobble rib
Work rib and bobble patt from chart working bobble thus:
(k1, yon, k1) into same st, turn.
P1, p1 tbl, p1, turn.
Knit into front and back of all 3 sts, do not turn.
Pass all sts one at a time over first st.

Intarsia hearts
Work colour patt from charts A or B as instructions. Read RS rows from R to L and WS rows from L to R.

Back
Using smaller needles and colour A cast on 96[108:116] sts. Start and work in bobble rib as chart, setting patt by commencing on st 2[5:1], counting st 1 as bottom right of diagram.
Continue in bobble rib as set until work measures 4in (10cm).
Change to larger needles and, starting with a knit row, start and work from chart A.
Work 54[52:52] rows of patt ending with RS facing.

Shape armholes
Keeping colour patt correct, cast off 4[4:5] sts at beg of next 2 rows. Dec 1 st at each end of next 1[3:5] rows, work 1 row. Dec 1 st at each end of next and every foll alt row until 70[76:80] sts.
Cont in patt until 1 complete repeat + 34 rows (i.e. ending at top of large heart on chart row 34) have been worked.
Cont in A and st st for rest of back and work in st st until armhole measures 8[8½:8¾]in (20[21.5:22]cm) ending with WS row.

Shape shoulders
Cast off 6[6:7] sts at beg of next 2 rows. Cast off 6[7:7] sts at beg of next 4 rows. Slip rem 34[36:38] sts on to a stitch holder.

Left Front
Using smaller needles and colour A cast on 48[54:57] sts. Start and work in bobble rib as chart, setting patt by commencing on st 2[5:1].
Continue in bobble rib as set until work measures 4in (10cm).

Change to larger needles and starting with a knit row start and work in st st and intarsia patt as chart A, but work so that centre of chart is first centre front st of patt – reversing patt for second front. Work 54[52:52] rows of patt ending with RS facing. (Work 1 extra row for R front.)

Shape armhole
Keeping colour patt correct, cast off 4[4:5] sts at beg of next row, work 1 row. Dec 1 st at armhole edge on next 1[3:5] rows, work 1 row. Dec 1 st at armhole edge of next and every foll alt row until 35[38:40] sts. Work until front measures 4½[5:4½]in (12[12.5:12]cm) ending at centre front edge.

Shape front neck
Keeping patt correct as set (and as given for back – i.e. finishing after chart row 34) cast off 6[7:6] sts at beg of next row, work 1 row. Cast off 3 sts at neck edge on next row. Dec 1 st at neck edge on next 3 rows.
Dec 1 st at neck edge on next and every alt row until 18[20:21] sts rem. Work until front measures same as back at shoulder shaping, ending at side edge.

Shape shoulder
Cast off 6[6:7] sts at beg of next row, work 1 row. Cast off 6[7:7] sts at beg of next and foll alt row.

Right Front
Work as given for L front, reversing col patt and noting difference in rows (at armhole) to reverse shaping.

Sleeves
Using smaller needles and colour A cast on 45 sts. Start and work in bobble rib as chart
(5 horizontal repeats) until sleeve measures 4in (10cm).
Change to larger needles and starting with a knit row start and work in st st and intarsia patt as chart B inc 1[2:2] sts on first row 46[48:48] sts. Work 2 rows. Inc 1 st (keeping patt correct) on next and every foll 6th[5th:4th] rows until 72[78:88] sts. Work straight until sleeve measures 19[19½:20]in (49[50:51]cm) from beg

Shape top

Cast off 4[4:5] sts at beg of next 2 rows, 64[70:78] sts. Dec 1 st at each end of next 6[7:7] rows. 52[56:64] sts. Work 2 rows. Dec 1 st at each end of next and every foll 3 rows 4[5:2] times in all, work 1 row. Dec 1 st at each end of next and every foll alt row until 32[34:44] sts rem. Dec 1 st at each end of next 5[5:9] rows. Cast off rem 22[24:26] sts.

Finishing

Tidy loose ends back into their own colours. Block pieces to correct measurements. Do not block ribs.

Button band

Using smaller needles and colour A with RS facing, pick up and k110 sts.
Row 1: p2, *k2, p2 rep from * to end. Work 5 more rows in 2 x 2 rib and cast off in rib.

Buttonhole band

Work as given for button band adding 6 evenly spaced buttonholes on 3rd rib row by casting off 2 sts where buttonhole required on this row and then casting on in the same position on 4th row.
Work 2 more rib rows and cast off in rib.

Collar

Join shoulder seams.
Using smaller needles and colour A, with RS facing pick up and knit 22[25:28] sts from halfway across front band along front neck to shoulder, 34[36:38] sts from stitch holder at back neck and 21[24:27] sts along front neck to halfway along front band, 77[85:93] sts.
Place a marker on centre st.
Inc row: k2 p3 (m1, k2) 16[18:20] times, k3 (2nd should have been marked st), (k2, m1) 16[18:20] times, p3, k2, 109[121:133] sts.
Commencing on st 9[3:6] and 2nd row (WS) of bobble rib chart, start and work in bobble rib until 7 bobbles and 1 row have been worked.
Using larger needle cast off in rib.
Set in sleeves.
Join side and sleeve seams, sewing ribs using a flat seam.
Sew on buttons to correspond with buttonholes. Steam seams.

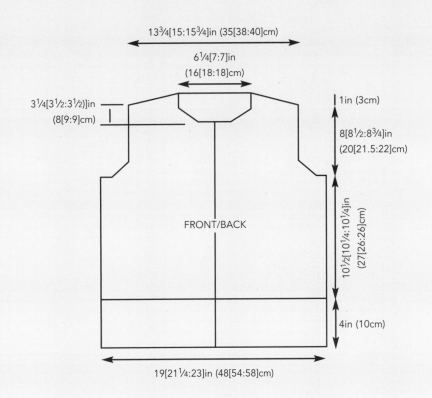

13¾[15:15¾]in (35[38:40]cm)

6¼[7:7]in (16[18:18]cm)

3¼[3½:3½)]in (8[9:9]cm)

1in (3cm)

8[8½:8¾]in (20[21.5:22]cm)

FRONT/BACK

10½[10¼:10¼]in (27[26:26]cm)

4in (10cm)

19[21¼:23]in (48[54:58]cm)

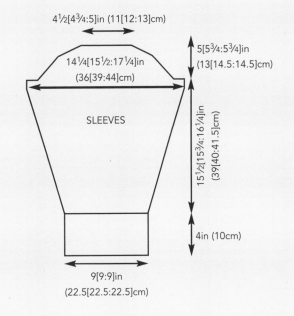

4½[4¾:5]in (11[12:13]cm)

14¼[15½:17¼]in (36[39:44]cm)

5[5¾:5¾]in (13[14.5:14.5]cm)

SLEEVES

15½[15¾:16¼]in (39[40:41.5]cm)

4in (10cm)

9[9:9]in (22.5[22.5:22.5]cm)

Pattern chart A Centre 46 sts x 72 rows

40in (102cm) 38in (96cm) 36in (91cm)   36in (91cm) 38in (96cm) 40in (102cm)

for patt repeats on back

← Start position   End position →

1 square = 1 st and 1 row Key ☐ A ■ B

Pattern chart B

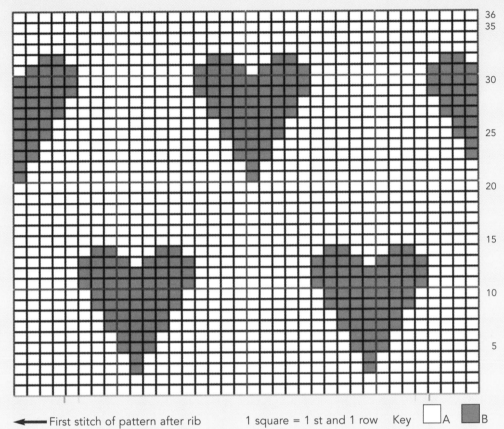

←── First stitch of pattern after rib   1 square = 1 st and 1 row   Key ☐A ▨B

Bobble rib 36 sts x 4 row repeat

1 square = 1 st and 1 row

Key

☐ st st k1 row, p1 row

• k on a purl row and p on a knit row

● Bobble

Main image page 23

Poppy

A childhood memory of intense red poppies in cornfields sparked off this classic floral cardigan design.

SIZES
To fit bust 32[34:37:40:44]in (81[86:94:101:112]cm)
See schematic for actual measurements

MATERIALS
UK Alpaca DK 290yd (265m) per 100g ball
3(4:4:5:5) balls colour A: Fawn
1(1:1:1:1) balls colour B: Rose
1(1:1:1:1) balls colour C: Black
1(1:1:1:1) balls colour D: Parchment
Needles: 1 pair 3.25mm (US 4)
Stitch holders
Buttons: 7 x ½in (1.5cm)

TENSION
24 sts and 32 rows = 4in (10cm) measured over pattern using 3.25mm (US 4) needles

STITCHES USED
Garter stitch (page 144)
Stocking stitch (page 144)

KNITTING NOTES
Note different starting positions for the 40 sts repeating pattern for different sizes and pieces.

Bell frill (US Bell ruffle)
Cast on a multiple of 9 sts plus 2.
Row 1: P2, *k7, p2 rep from * to end.
Row 2: K2 *p7, k2 rep from * to end.
Row 3: P2, *sl 1, k1, psso, k3, k2tog, p2 rep from * to end.
Row 4: K2 *p5, k2, rep from * to end.
Row 5: P2, *sl 1, k1, psso, k1, k2tog, p2, rep from * to end.
Row 6: K2 *p3, k2, rep from * to end.
Row 7: P2, *sl 1, k2tog, psso, p2 rep from * to end.
Row 8: K2, *p1, k2, rep from * to end.

Back
Using needles and colour A cast on 326[344:362:380:398] sts. Work the 8 rows of frill** 110[116:122:128:134] sts. Start and work in the **woven intarsia** technique (described on page 148), until back measures 11[11:11:12:12]in (28[28:28:30:30]cm) from beg***.

Shape armholes
Cast off 5[6:6:6:7] sts at beg of next 2 rows. Cast off 3 sts at beg of next 2 rows. Cast off 2[2:3:3:3] sts at beg of next 2 rows. Dec 1 st at each end of next and every foll alt row until 80[84:88:94:96] sts rem. Work straight until armhole measures 7½[8:8:8½:9]in (19[20:21:22:23.5]cm) ending with WS row.

Shape neck and shoulder
Cast off 5[5:6:6:6] sts, work across next 20[22:22:25:25] sts, note position in patt sequence, turn and cont on these sts for first side. Dec 1 st at beg (neck edge) of next 5[4:4:4:4] rows and at the same time, work to shoulder edge and cast off 5[6:6:7:7] sts at beg of next and every foll alt row until all sts cast off. RS facing, slip next 30[30:32:32:34] sts on to a stitch holder, rejoin yarn to rem sts and work from noted position to end. Cast off 5 sts at beg and dec 1 st at end of next row. Dec 1 st at neck edge of next 4[3:3:3:3] rows and at the same time, work to shoulder edge and cast off 5[6:6:7:7] sts at beg of next and every foll alt row until all sts cast off.

Right Front
Using needles and colour A cast on 164[173:182:191:200] sts and work as given for back to ** dec 1[2:2:2:2]sts at end(s) of last row to give 55[57:60:63:66] sts. Work as given for back from ** to ***, 55[57:60:63:66] sts ending at armhole edge.

Shape armhole
Cast off 5[6:6:6:7] sts at beg of next row, work 1 row. Cast off 3 sts at beg of next row, work 1 row. Cast off 2[2:3:3:3] sts at beg of next row, work 1 row. Dec 1 st at armhole edge of next and every foll alt row until 40[42:44:47:48] sts rem. Work straight until armhole measures 5[5½:6:6:6½]in (13[14:15:15:16]cm) ending at neck edge.

Shape neck
Cast off 11[11:12:12:13] sts at neck edge on next row, work 1 row. Cast off 2 sts at neck edge on next and foll alt row, work 1 row. Dec 1 st at neck edge on next and every foll alt row until 21[23:24:27:27] sts rem. Work straight until armhole matches back, ending at armhole edge.

Shape shoulder
Cast off 5[5:6:6:6] sts, at beg of next row, work 1 row. Cast off 5[6:6:7:7] sts at beg of next and every foll alt row until all sts cast off.

Left Front
Work as given for R front reversing shaping.

Sleeves
Using needles and colour A cast on 218[218:227:227:245] sts and work as for back to ** dec[dec:dec:dec:inc] as necessary to obtain 72[72:76:76:82] sts. Start and work in patt from chart and work 2 rows. Inc 1 st at each end of next and every foll 12th[12th:12th:10th:12th] row until 82[86:88:94:98] sts. Work straight until sleeve measures 11[11:12:12:12½]in (28[28:30:30:32]cm) ending with WS row.

Shape top

Cast off 5[5:6:6:6] sts at beg of next 2 rows. Dec 1 st at each end of next and every foll alt row 14[14:16:15:17] times, work 1 row. Dec 1 st at each end of every row until 20 sts rem. Cast off.

Finishing

Tidy loose ends back into their own colours. Block pieces to correct measurements.

Button band

RS facing, using colour B, pick up and knit 9 sts from every 10 rows, knit 4 rows and cast off. Place 7 evenly spaced markers on band.

Buttonhole band

Pick up same number of sts as for button band. Work as for button band, but on 2nd knit row, when matching marker positions reached, make buttonholes by casting off 2 sts for each buttonhole on next row and then casting on 2 sts over those cast off on foll row. Knit 1 row and cast off.

Neck band

Join shoulder seams. Using B and RS facing, starting halfway across the top edge of the front band, pick up and knit approx 32[32:34:36:38] sts along front neck, 4 sts from back side neck, 30[30:32:32:34] sts from back stitch holder, 4 sts from back side neck, 32[32:34:36:38] sts along rem front neck. Work 4 rows garter stitch and cast off.

Set in sleeves. Join side and sleeve seams. Sew on buttons to correspond with buttonholes. Steam seams.

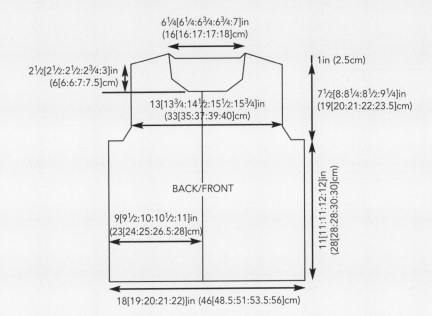

6¼[6¼:6¾:6¾:7]in
(16[16:17:17:18]cm)

1in (2.5cm)

2½[2½:2½:2¾:3]in
(6[6:6:7:7.5]cm)

7½[8:8¼:8½:9¼]in
(19[20:21:22:23.5]cm)

13[13¾:14½:15½:15¾]in
(33[35:37:39:40]cm)

BACK/FRONT

11[11:11:12:12]in
(28[28:28:30:30]cm)

9[9½:10:10½:11]in
(23[24:25:26.5:28]cm)

18[19:20:21:22])in (46[48.5:51:53.5:56]cm)

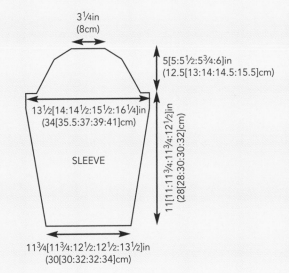

3¼in
(8cm)

5[5:5½:5¾:6]in
(12.5[13:14:14.5:15.5]cm)

13½[14:14½:15½:16¼]in
(34[35.5:37:39:41]cm)

SLEEVE

11[11:11¾:11¾:12½]in
(28[28:30:30:32]cm)

11¾[11¾:12½:12½:13½]in
(30[30:32:32:34]cm)

Pattern chart

40 sts x 80 rows

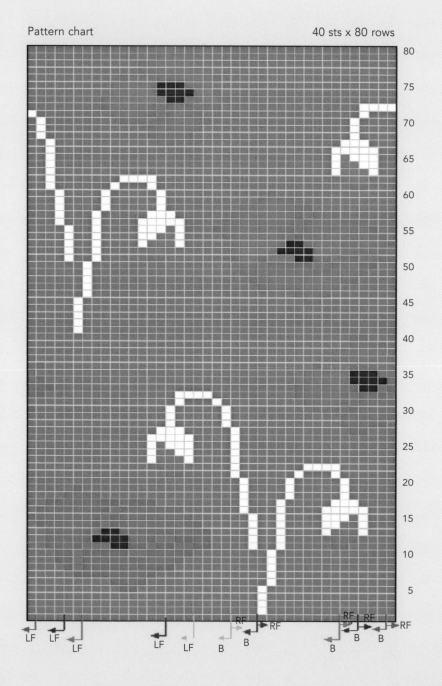

1 square = 1 st and 1 row

Key

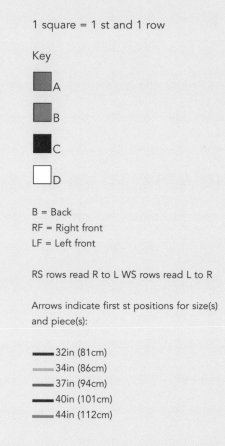

A

B

C

D

B = Back
RF = Right front
LF = Left front

RS rows read R to L WS rows read L to R

Arrows indicate first st positions for size(s)
and piece(s):

32in (81cm)
34in (86cm)
37in (94cm)
40in (101cm)
44in (112cm)

Main image page 24

Rosebud

Alternating vertical panels of lace and roses blend effortlessly to make a flattering summer jacket. The moss stitch belt accentuates the fitted waistline.

SIZES
To fit 32[34:36:38:40]in
(81[86:91:97:102]cm)
See schematic for actual measurements

MATERIALS
Rowan wool/cotton
123yd (113m) per 50g ball
8[9:9:10:10] balls colour A:
    Hiss (952)
2[2:2:2:2] balls colour B:
    Tender (951)
2[2:2:2:2] balls colour C:
    Flower (943)
2[2:2:2:2] balls colour D:
    Riviera (930)
2[2:2:2:2] balls colour E:
    Deepest Olive (907)
Needles: 1 pair each 3.25mm (US 3) and 4mm (US 6)
Stitch holder
Buttons: 9 x ½in (1.5cm)

TENSION
24 sts and 30 rows = 4in (10 cm) measured over lace and st st pattern using larger needles.

STITCHES USED
Stocking stitch (page 144)
Moss (seed) stitch (page 144)
Little Vine Lace Pattern (page 134)

Back
Using smaller needles and colour A cast on 103[109:115:121:127] sts
Row 1: (RS) K1, *p1, k1, rep from * to end.
Row 2: As row 1.
These 2 rows form moss st (seed stitch). Work in moss st for a further 6 rows, inc 1 st at end of last row and ending with a WS row.
104[110:116:122:128] sts.
Change to larger needles.
Using the **woven intarsia** technique (described on page 148) starting and ending rows as indicated and repeating the 32 row repeat throughout, cont in patt from chart for back as folls:
Dec 1 st at each end of 5th and every foll 6th row until 92[98:104:110:116] sts rem.
Work 15 rows, ending with a WS row.
Inc 1 st at each end of next and every foll 8th row until there are 104[110:116:122:128] sts, taking inc sts into patt.
Cont straight until back measures 14½[15:15:15½:15½]in (37[38:38:39:39]cm), ending with a WS row.
Shape armholes
Keeping patt correct, cast off 3[4:4:5:5] sts at beg of next 2 rows.
98[102:108:112:118] sts.
Dec 1 st at each end of next 3[3:5:5:7] rows, then on foll 1[2:2:3:3] alt rows, then on foll 4th row.
88[90:92:94:96] sts.
Cont straight until armhole measures 8[8:8¼:8¼:8¾]in (20[20:21:21:22]cm), ending with a WS row.
Shape shoulders and back neck
Cast off 8[8:9:9:9] sts at beg of next 2 rows. 72[74:74:76:78] sts.
Next row: (RS) Cast off 8[8:9:9:9] sts, patt until there are 13[13:12:12:13] sts on right needle and turn, leaving rem sts on a holder.
Work each side of neck separately.
Cast off 4 sts at beg of next row.
Cast off rem 9[9:8:8:9] sts.
With RS facing, rejoin yarn to rem sts, cast off centre 30[32:32:34:34] sts, patt to end.
Complete to match first side, reversing shapings.

Left Front
Using smaller needles and colour A cast on 55[57:61:63:67] sts
Work in moss st as given for back for 7 rows, ending with a RS row.
Row 8: (WS) Moss st 7 sts and slip these sts onto a holder, m1, moss st to last 0[1:0:1:0] st, (inc in last st) 0[1:0:1:0] times.
49[52:55:58:61] sts.
Change to larger needles.
Starting and ending rows as indicated, cont in patt from chart for left front as folls:
Dec 1 st at beg of 5th and every foll 6th row until 43[46:49:52:55] sts rem.
Work 15 rows, ending with a WS row.
Inc 1 st at beg of next and every foll 8th row until there are 49[52:55:58:61] sts, taking inc sts into patt.
Cont straight until left front matches back to beg of armhole shaping, ending with a WS row.
Shape armhole
Keeping patt correct, cast off 3[4:4:5:5] sts at beg of next row.
46[48:51:53:56] sts.
Work 1 row.
Dec 1 st at armhole edge of next 3[3:5:5:7] rows, then on foll 1[2:2:3:3] alt rows, then on foll 4th row.
41[42:43:44:45] sts.
Cont straight until 15[15:15:17:17] rows less have been worked than on back to start of shoulder shaping, ending with a RS row.
Shape neck
Keeping patt correct, cast off 5[6:6:6:6] sts at beg of next row, then 4 sts at beg of foll alt row.
32[32:33:34:35] sts.
Dec 1 st at neck edge of next 5 rows, then on foll 2[2:2:3:3] alt rows.
25[25:26:26:27] sts.
Work 3 rows, ending with a WS row.
Shape shoulder
Cast off 8[8:9:9:9] sts at beg of next and foll alt row.
Work 1 row.
Cast off rem 9[9:8:8:9] sts.

Right Front
Using smaller needles and colour A cast on 55[57:61:63:67] sts
Work in moss st as given for back for 4 rows, ending with a WS row.

Row 5: (buttonhole row) (RS) K1, p1, k2tog, yfwd, moss st to end.
Work in moss st for a further 2 rows, ending with a RS row.
Row 8: (WS) (Inc in first st) 0[1:0:1:0] times, moss st to last 7 sts, m1 and turn, leaving rem 7 sts on a holder. 49[52:55:58:61] sts.
Change to larger needles.
Starting and ending rows as indicated, cont in patt from chart for right front as folls:
Dec 1 st at end of 5th and every foll 6th row until 43[46:49:52:55] sts rem.
Complete as given for left front, following chart for right front and reversing shapings.

Sleeves

Using smaller needles and colour A cast on 55[55:57:59:59] sts.
Work in moss st as given for back for 8 rows, inc 1 st at end of last row and ending with a WS row.
56[56:58:60:60] sts.
Change to larger needles.
Starting and ending rows as indicated, cont in patt from chart for sleeves, shaping sides by inc 1 st at each end of 7th and every foll 8th row to 66 [76:76:78:88] sts, then on every foll 10th [10th:10th:10th:0] row until there are 80[82:84:86:88] sts.
Cont straight until sleeve measures 17¼[17¼:17¾:17¾:17¾]in (44[44:45:45:45]cm), ending with a WS row.

Shape top
Keeping patt correct, cast off 3[4:4:5:5] sts at beg of next 2 rows.
74[74:76:76:78] sts.
Dec 1 st at each end of next 5 rows, then on foll 2 alt rows, then on every foll 4th row until 54[54:56:56:58] sts rem.
Work 1 row, ending with a WS row.
Dec 1 st at each end of next and every foll alt row to 46 sts, then on foll 3 rows, ending with a WS row.
Cast off 6 sts at beg of next 4 rows.
Cast off rem 16 sts.

Finishing

Tidy loose ends back into their own colours. Block pieces to correct measurements.

Button band
Slip 7 sts left on left front holder onto smaller needles and rejoin yarn A with RS facing.
Cont in moss st as set until band, when slightly stretched, fits up left front opening edge to neck shaping, ending with a WS row.
Break yarn and leave sts on a holder.
Slip stitch band in position.
Mark positions for 9 buttons on this band – first to come level with buttonhole already worked in right front, last to come ½in (1cm) up from neck shaping and rem 7 buttons evenly spaced between.

Buttonhole band
Slip 7 sts left on right front holder onto smaller needles and rejoin yarn A with WS facing.
Cont in moss st as set until band, when slightly stretched, fits up right front opening edge to neck shaping, ending with a WS row and with the addition of a further 7 buttonholes worked as folls:

Buttonhole row: (RS) K1, p1, k2tog, yfwd, k1, p1, k1.
Do NOT break off yarn. Slip stitch band in position.
Join shoulder seams.

Neckband
With RS facing, using smaller needles and colour A, moss st across 7 sts of buttonhole band, pick up and knit 23[24:24:27:27] sts up right side of neck, 39[41:41:43:43] sts from back, and 23[24:24:27:27] sts down left side of neck, then moss st across 7 sts of button band.
99[103:103:111:111] sts.
Work in moss st as set by front bands for 2 rows, ending with a RS row.
Row 3: (WS) Moss st to last 4 sts, yfwd (to make 9th buttonhole), k2tog tbl, moss st to end.
Work in moss st for a further 2 rows.
Cast off in moss st.

Belt
Using smaller needles and colour A cast on 7 sts
Work in moss st as given for back until belt measures 53¾in (135cm),
Cast off.
Join side seams and sleeve seams.
Set sleeves into armholes.
Sew on buttons to correspond with buttonholes.
Steam seams.

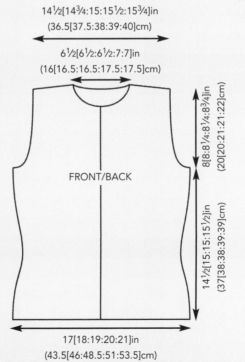

14½[14¾:15:15½:15¾]in
(36.5[37.5:38:39:40]cm)

6½[6½:6½:7:7]in
(16[16.5:16.5:17.5:17.5]cm)

FRONT/BACK

8[8:8¼:8¼:8¾]in
(20[20:21:21:22]cm)

14½[15:15:15:15½]in
(37[38:38:39:39]cm)

17[18:19:20:21]in
(43.5[46:48.5:51:53.5]cm)

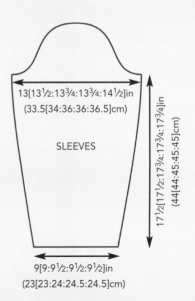

13[13½:13¾:13¾:14½]in
(33.5[34:36:36:36.5]cm)

SLEEVES

17½[17½:17¾:17¾:17¾]in
(44[44:45:45:45]cm)

9[9:9½:9½:9½]in
(23[23:24:24.5:24.5]cm)

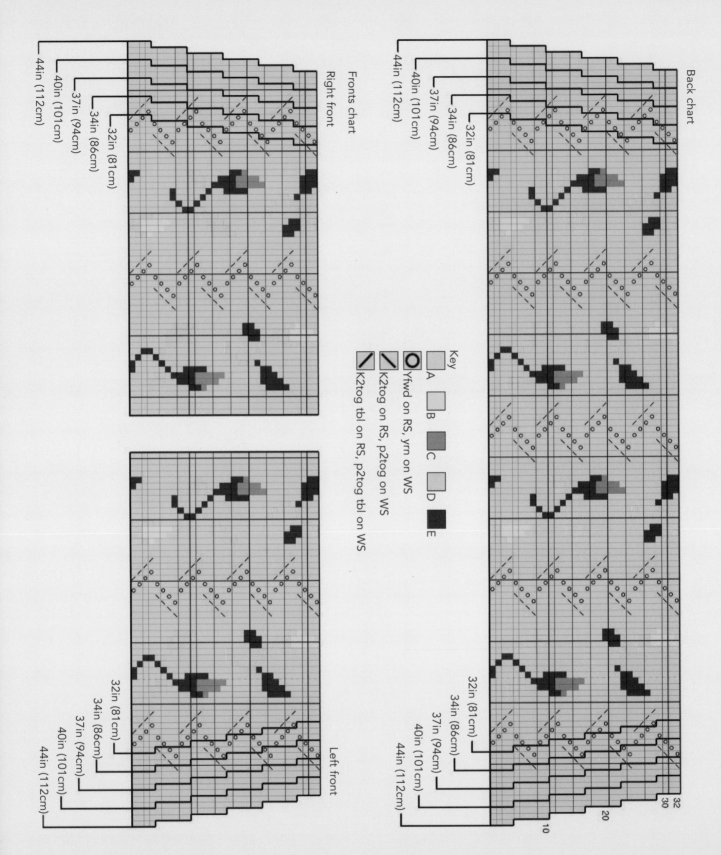

Back chart

44in (112cm)
40in (101cm)
37in (94cm)
34in (86cm)
32in (81cm)

Fronts chart

Right front

44in (112cm)
40in (101cm)
37in (94cm)
34in (86cm)
32in (81cm)

Key

A
B
C
D
E

◯ Yfwd on RS, yrn on WS
╱ K2tog on RS, p2tog on WS
╲ K2tog tbl on RS, p2tog tbl on WS

32in (81cm)
34in (86cm)
37in (94cm)
40in (101cm)
44in (112cm)

Left front

32in (81cm)
34in (86cm)
37in (94cm)
40in (101cm)
44in (112cm)

10
20
30
32

Sleeve chart

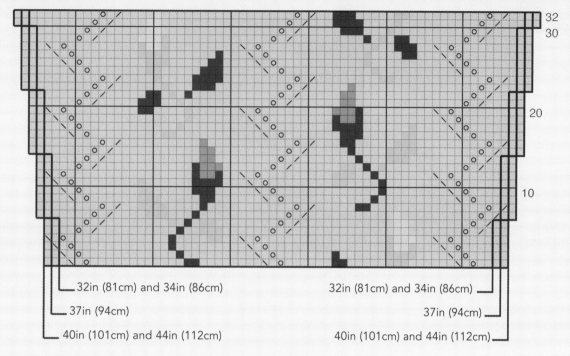

32
30

20

10

32in (81cm) and 34in (86cm)   32in (81cm) and 34in (86cm)

37in (94cm)   37in (94cm)

40in (101cm) and 44in (112cm)   40in (101cm) and 44in (112cm)

Pink colourway image page 29

Turquoise colourway image page 28

Pebble

A painting of pebbles on the beach was the starting point for this easy two-colour top. The subtle colour variations are dyed into the yarn, making this crossover piece a year-round wardrobe classic.

SIZES
To fit bust 32(34:37:40:44)in
81[86:94:101:112]cm)
See schematic for actual measurements

MATERIALS
Pink colourway
Rowan Felted Tweed
191yd (175m) per 50g ball
4[5:5:6:7] balls colour A:
 Treacle (145)
Rowan Tapestry
131yd (120m) per 50g ball
4[5:6:7:8] balls colour B:
 Pot Pourri (172)

Turquoise colourway
Rowan Felted Tweed
4[5:5:6:7] balls colour A:
 Turquoise (152)
Rowan Tapestry
4[5:6:7:8] balls colour B:
 Moorland (175)

Needles: 1 pair each 3.25mm (US 4) and 4mm (US 6)
Circular needle
Stitch holder

TENSION
22 sts and 30 rows = 4in (10cm) measured over pattern using arger needles.

STITCHES USED
Stocking stitch (page 144)
Moss (seed) stitch (page 144)
Woven intarsia (page 148)

TIPS
Use yarn B continuously, keeping small balls or bobbins of yarn A in appropriate places. Weave B behind A at all times.

Note: Side seam of pattern does not match or mirror.

Back
Using smaller needles and colour A, cast on 100[106:112:116:120] sts and work in moss st for ¾in (2cm).
Change to larger needles.
Work col patt from chart, using the **woven intarsia** technique (described on page 148), placing patt thus:
Start on 15th[18th:21st:23rd:25th] st from L of chart. Cont throughout in patt as set and at the same time, dec 1 st at each end of 11th and every foll 8th row until 94[100:106:110:114] sts, then on every foll 6th row until 88[94:100:104:108] sts rem. Work straight until back measures 12in (25cm), ending with RS facing for next row. Inc 1 st at each end of next and foll 8th row, then on every foll 10th row until there are 100[106:112:116:120]

sts, taking inc sts into pattern.
Work straight until piece measures 15½[15:14½:14:13¾]in (39[38:37:36:35]cm) ending with RS facing for next row.
Shape armholes
Cast off 5[6:6:7:7] sts at beg of next 2 rows. Dec 1 st at each end of next 3[4:5:5:5] rows, then on foll 3[3:4:4:4] alt rows, then on every foll 4th row until 74[76:78:80:82] sts rem. Work straight until armhole measures 8¼[8¾:9:9½:9¾]in (21[22:23:24:25]cm) ending with RS facing for next row.
Shape shoulders
Cast off 7 sts at beg of next 2 rows.
Next row: (RS) Cast off 7[7:7:8:8] sts, patt until there are 11[12:12:12:12] sts on R needle and turn, leaving rem sts on a holder. Work each side of neck separately.
Cast off 4 sts at beg of next row. Cast off rem 7[8:8:8:8] sts.
With RS facing, rejoin yarn to rem sts, cast off centre 24[24:26:26:28] sts, patt to end. Complete to match first side, reversing shapings.

Right Front
Using smaller needles and colour A cast on 74[80:86:90:94] sts and work in moss st for ¾in (2cm).
Change to larger needles. Start and work in patt from chart, all sizes commencing on st 1 of chart on R and read RS rows from R to L and WS rows from L to R. Keeping patt correct as set, shape side seam by dec 1st at side edge on 11th and every foll 8th row until 71[77:83:87:91] sts, then on every foll 6th row until 68[74:80:84:88] sts rem. Work straight until 6 rows less have been worked than on back to first side seam dec, ending with RS facing for next row.
Shape neck
Dec 1 st at neck edge of next and foll 19[22:26:28:33] alt rows, then on 4 foll 4th rows and at same time inc 1 st at side seam edge on 7th and foll 8th row, then on every foll 10th row 4 times, taking inc sts into patt. Dec 1 st at neck edge only on 4th and every foll 4th row. At the same time, when front measures same as back to armhole shaping, ending at armhole edge.

Shape armhole

Cast off 5[6:6:7:7] sts at beg of next row, work 1 row. Dec 1 st at armhole edge of next 3[4:5:5:5] rows, then on foll 3[3:4:4:4] alt rows, then on next 2[2:2:2:3] foll 4th rows. Keep dec at neck edge as set until 21[22:22:23:23] sts rem. Work straight until front matches back to beg of shoulder shaping, ending at armhole edge.

Shape shoulder

Cast off 7 sts at beg of next row, work 1 row. Cast off 7[7:7:8:8] sts, at beg of next row, work 1 row. Cast off rem 7[8:8:8:8] sts.

Left Front

Using smaller needles and colour A cast on 74[80:86:90:94] sts and work in moss st for ¾in (2cm).
Change to larger needles. Start and work in patt from chart, all sizes commencing on st 1 of chart on L and read RS rows from L to R and WS rows from R to L. Work as given for R front reversing all shaping by working an extra row before beg of armhole and shoulder shaping.

Sleeves

Using smaller needles and colour A cast on 48 sts. Work in moss st for ¾in (2cm), inc 1 st at end of last row. (49 sts.) Change to larger needles and work in st st throughout. Work 2 rows. Inc 1 st at each end of next and every foll 8th row until 74[76:78:80:82] sts. Work straight until sleeve measures approx 17½[17¾:17¾:18:18]in (44.5[45:45:46:46]cm) ending with RS facing.

Shape top

Cast off 5[6:6:7:7] sts at beg of next 2 rows. Dec 1 st at each end of foll 20[22:23:21:16] alt rows then on every 3rd[0:0:3rd:3rd] rows, until 20 sts. Cast off.

Finishing

Tidy loose ends back into their own colours. Block to correct measurements. Join shoulder seams.

Front band

With RS facing, using smaller circular needle and colour A, start at cast-on edge and pick up and knit 42 sts up

R front opening edge to beg of front slope shaping 95[97:99:103:105] sts up R front slope to shoulder, 32[32:34:34:36] sts from back, 95[97:99:103:105] sts down L front slope to beg of front slope shaping, then 42 sts down L front opening edge to cast-on edge

306[310:316:324:330] sts. Work in moss st for 6 rows.
Cast off loosely in moss st. Join sleeve seams and side seams, leave a small opening in R side seam level with beg of front slope shaping. Set in sleeves. Steam seams.

(continued overleaf)

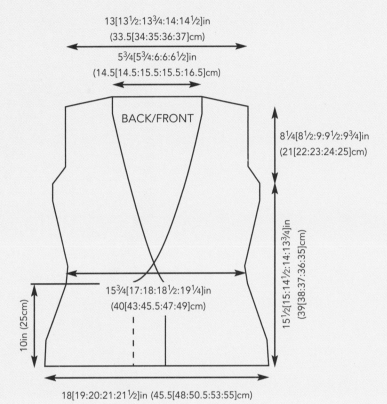

13[13½:13¾:14:14½]in
(33.5[34:35:36:37]cm)

5¾[5¾:6:6:6½]in
(14.5[14.5:15.5:15.5:16.5]cm)

BACK/FRONT

8¼[8½:9:9½:9¾]in
(21[22:23:24:25]cm)

15½[15:14½:14:13¾]in
(39[38:37:36:35]cm)

15¾[17:18:18½:19¼]in
(40[43:45.5:47:49]cm)

10in (25cm)

18[19:20:21:21½]in (45.5[48:50.5:53:55]cm)

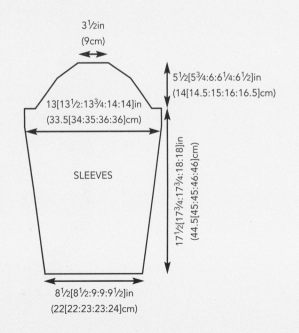

3½in
(9cm)

13[13½:13¾:14:14]in
(33.5[34:35:36:36]cm)

5½[5¾:6:6¼:6½]in
(14[14.5:15:16:16.5]cm)

SLEEVES

17½[17¾:17¾:18:18]in
(44.5[45:45:46:46]cm)

8½[8½:9:9:9½]in
(22[22:23:23:24]cm)

Ties (make 2)

Using smaller needles and colour A
loosely cast on 110 sts and work 4
rows moss st. Cast off in moss st.
Attach ties to R and L fronts at end of
front slope shaping. Make 2 x 4in (5 x
10cm) long tassels with B and attach
to ends of ties.

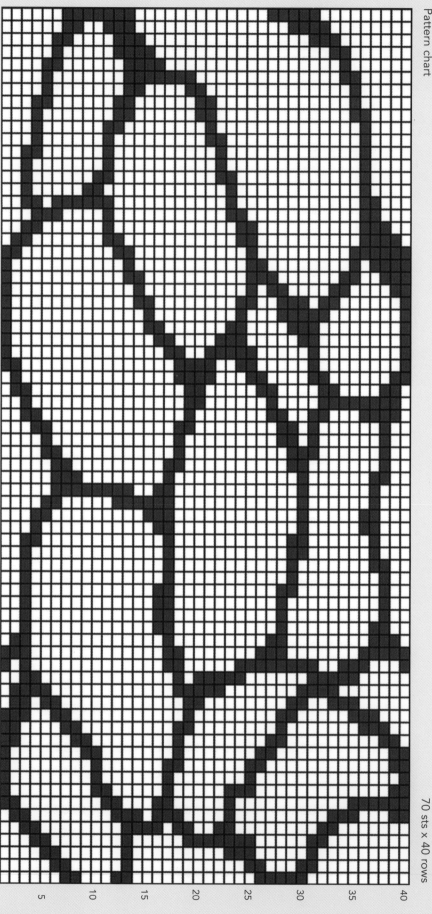

Pink colourway
1 square = 1 st and 1 row

Key
■ A
□ B

Work RS rows from R to L and WS rows from L to R

70 sts x 40 rows

Pattern chart

70 sts x 40 rows

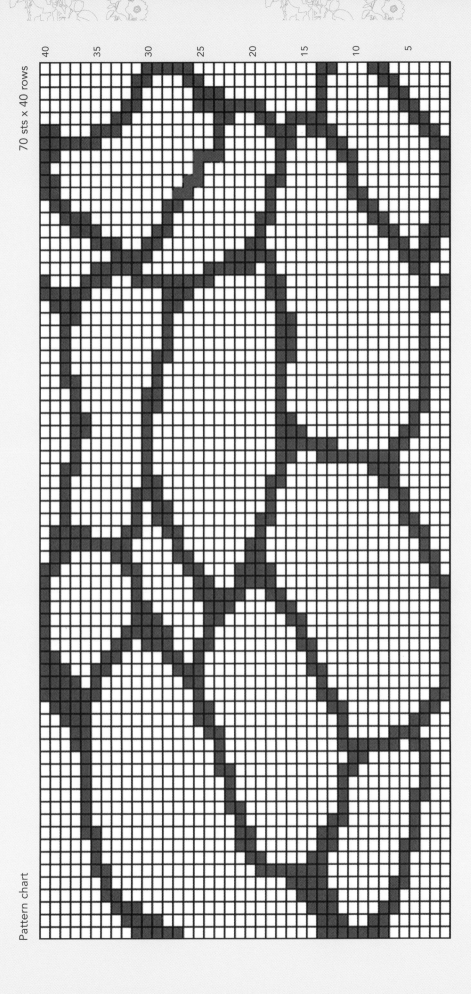

Turquoise colourway
1 square = 1 st and 1 row

Key

A ▢B

Work RS rows from R to L and WS rows from L to R

Main image page 30

Tiny Flower

This subtle design juxtaposes flowers with patterns of tiny cables. The delicate crochet trim at neck, cuffs and welt accents the femininity of the piece.

SIZES

To fit 32[34:36:38:40]in (81[86:91:97:102]cm)
See schematic on page 90 for actual measurements

MATERIALS

Rowan Scottish Tweed 4-ply 120yd (110m) per 25g ball
11[11:12:12:13] balls colour A:
    Sea Green 06
2[2:2:3:3] balls colour B:
    Machair 02
1[1:1:1:1] ball colour C:
    Lavender 14
Rowan wool cotton 123yd (113m) per 50g ball
1[1:1:1:1] ball colour D:
    Pumpkin 962
Jaeger silk 137yd (125m) per 50g ball
1[1:1:1:1] ball colour E:
    Dawn 02
1[1:1:1:1] ball colour F:
    Cameo 08
Needles: 1 pair each 2.25mm (US 1) and 3mm (US 2/3) cable needle, 2.5mm (US C2) crochet hook
Buttons: 9 x ⅜in (1cm)
Stitch holder

TENSION

28 sts and 40 rows = 4in (10cm) measured over cable and st st pattern using larger needles.

STITCHES USED

Stocking stitch (page 144)
Garter stitch (page 144)
C4B (page 145)
Crochet slip stitch (page 152)
Crochet chain (page 152)
Double/treble crochet (page 153)

KNITTING NOTES

Partial flowers can be worked to accommodate the different start and end positions for your size. When partial cables come into pattern, work them in st st.

Back

Using larger needles and colour A cast on 124[130:138:144:152] sts, using the **woven intarsia** technique (described on page 148), starting and ending rows thus:
Commence chart on st 3L[5L, 9L, 12L, 16L] rep chart (R to L) to end.
Cont in patt as set working the 80 row patt repeat of chart throughout, and work as follows:
Work a further 7 rows, ending with WS row.
Dec 1 st at each end of next and every foll 6th row until 114[120:128:134:142] sts rem.
Work 17 rows, ending with a WS row.
Inc 1 st at each end of next and every foll 12th row until there are 124[130:138:144:152] sts, taking inc sts into patt.
Cont straight until back measures 11½[12:12:12¼:12¼]in (29[30:30:31:31]cm) ending with a WS row.
Shape armholes
Keeping patt correct, cast off 7[8:8:9:9] sts at beg of next 2 rows. 110[114:122:126:134] sts.
Dec 1 st at each end of next 5[5:7:7:9] rows, then on foll 1[2:2:3:3] alt rows then on every foll 4th row until 94[96:100:102:106] sts rem.
Cont straight until armhole measures 8[8:8¼:8¼:8¾]in (20[20:21:21:22]cm), ending with a WS row.

Shape shoulders and back neck

Cast off 8[8:9:9:10] sts at beg of next 2 rows 78[80:82:84:86]sts.
Next row: (RS) Cast off 8[8:9:9:10] sts, patt until there are 13 sts on right needle and turn, leaving rem sts on a holder.
Work each side of neck separately.
Cast off 4 sts at beg of next row.
Cast off rem 9 sts.
With RS facing, rejoin yarn to rem sts, cast off centre 36[38:38:40:40] sts, patt to end.
Complete to match first side, reversing shapings.

Left Front

Using larger needles and colour A cast on 64[67:71:74:78] sts.
Row 1: Commence on st 12L[13L:36L:37L:39L] work patt rep from chart (R to L) to end.
(Note: do NOT work part flower or cable motifs along front opening edge.)
Work a further 7 rows, ending with WS row.
Dec 1 st at beg of next and every foll 6th row until 59[62:66:69:73] rem.
Work 17 rows, ending with a WS row.
Inc 1 st at beg of next and every foll 12th row until there are 64[67:71:74:78] sts, taking inc sts into pattern.
Cont straight until left front matches back to beg of armhole shaping, ending with a WS row.
Shape armhole
Keeping patt correct, cast off 7[8:8:9:9] sts at beg of next row: 57[59:63:65:69] sts.
Work 1 row
Dec 1 st at armhole edge of next 5[5:7:7:9] rows, then on foll 1[2:2:3:3] alt rows, then on every foll 4th row until 49[50:52:53:55] sts rem.
Cont straight until 21[21:21:23:23] rows less have been worked than on back to start of shoulder shaping, ending with a RS row.
Shape neck
Keeping patt correct, cast off 9[10:10:10:10] sts at beg of next row, then 6 sts at beg of foll alt row. 34[34:36:37:39] sts.

Dec 1 st at neck edge of next 5 rows,

Dec 1 st at neck edge of next 5 rows, then on foll 3[3:3:4:4] alt rows, then on foll 4th row: 25[25:27:27:29] sts. Work 3 rows, ending with a WS row.

Shape shoulder
Cast off 8[8:9:9:10] sts at beg of next and foll alt row.
Work 1 row, cast off rem 9 sts.

Right Front
Using larger needles and colour A, cast on 64[67:71:74:78] sts starting rows as for L front.
(Note: do NOT work part flower or cable motifs along front opening edge.)
Work 8 rows ending with a WS row.
Dec 1 st at end of next and every foll 6th row until 59[62:66:69:73] sts rem.
Complete to match left front, reversing shapings.

Sleeves
Using larger needles and colour A cast on 64[64:66:68:68] sts.
Start and work in chart patt thus:
Row 1: Commence chart on st 12L[12L:13L:14L:14L] and repeating the 80 row repeat throughout. Cont in patt as set from chart, shaping sides by inc 1 st at each end of 7th and every foll 8th [8th:8th:8th:6th] row to 70[80:88:90:72] sts, then on every foll 10th[10th:10th:10th:8th] row until there are 94[96:100:102:106] sts, taking inc sts into patt.
Cont straight until sleeve measures 16[16:16½:16½:16½]in (41[41:42:42:42] cm) ending with a WS row.

Shape top
Keeping patt correct, cast off 7[8:8:9:9] sts at beg of next 2 rows, 80[80:84:84:88] sts.
Dec 1 st at each end of next 5 rows, then on foll 2 alt rows, then on every foll 4th row until 54[54:58:58:62] sts rem.
Work 1 row, ending with a WS row.
Dec 1 st at each end of next and every foll alt row to 42 sts, then on foll 7 rows, ending with a WS row.
Cast off rem 28 sts.

Finishing
Tidy loose ends back into their own colours. Block pieces to correct measurements.
Join both shoulder seams.

Button band
Using smaller needles and colour A and with RS facing, pick up and knit 127[127:127:135:135] sts evenly down left front opening edge, between neck shaping and cast on edge.
Work in garter st for 2 rows.
Cast off knit-wise (on WS).

Buttonhole band
Work to match button band, picking up sts up right front opening edge and with the addition of 6 buttonholes worked in row 2 as foll:
Row 2: (RS) K2, *K2tog, yfwd (to make a buttonhole), k13(13:13:14:14) rep from * to last 5 sts, K2tog, yfwd (to make 9th buttonhole), k3.

Neckband
With RS facing, using 2.5 mm (US C2) crochet hook and yarn B starting and ending at cast-off edge of bands, work a row of ss evenly around entire neck edge, working a multiple of 4 sts plus 1 st, turn.

Row 1:(WS): 1 ch (does NOT count as st), 1 dc into first st, *5 ch, miss 3 sts, 1 dc into next st, rep from * to end, turn.
Row 2: (2 dc, 3 ch, ss to last dc, 2 dc) into each ch sp to end, ending with ss to dc at beg of previous row.
Fasten off. Join side seams.

Hem edging
With RS facing, using 2.5 mm (US C2) crochet hook and yarn B starting and ending at cast-off edge of bands, work a row of ss evenly around entire hem edge, working a multiple of 4 sts plus 1 st, turn.
Row 1: (WS) 1 ch (does NOT count as st), 1 dc into first st, *5 ch, miss 3 sts, 1 dc into next st, rep from * to end, turn.
Row 2: 5 ch, 1 dc into first ch sp, * 5 ch, 1 dc into next ch sp, rep from * to end, 2 ch, 1 tr into dc at beg of previous row, turn.
Row 3: 1 ch (does NOT count as st), 1 dc into tr at end of previous row, *5 ch, 1 dc into next ch sp, rep from * to end, working last dc into 3rd of 5 ch at beg of previous row, turn.
Rows 4 to 7: As rows 2 and 3, twice.
Row 8: (2 dc, 3 ch, ss to last dc, 2 dc) into each ch sp to end, ending with ss to dc at beg of previous row.
Fasten off
In same way, work edging along cast-on edge of sleeves.
Set sleeves into armholes.
Join sleeve seams, sew on buttons to correspond with buttonholes.
Steam seams.

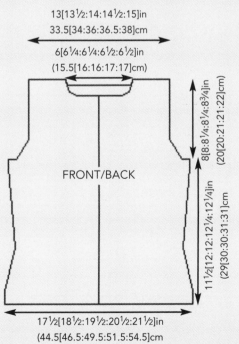

13[13½:14:14½:15]in
33.5[34:36:36.5:38]cm

6[6¼:6¼:6½:6½]in
(15.5[16:16:17:17]cm)

FRONT/BACK

8[8:8¼:8¼:8¾]in
(20[20:21:21:22]cm)

11½[12:12:12¼:12¼]in
(29[30:30:31:31]cm)

17½[18½:19½:20½:21½]in
(44.5[46.5:49.5:51.5:54.5]cm)

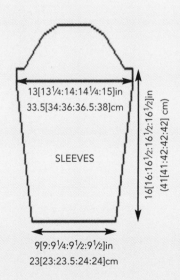

13[13¼:14:14¼:15]in
33.5[34:36:36.5:38]cm

SLEEVES

16[16:16½:16½:16½]in
(41[41:42:42:42] cm)

9[9:9¼:9½:9½]in
23[23:23.5:24:24]cm

Pattern chart

40 sts x 80 rows

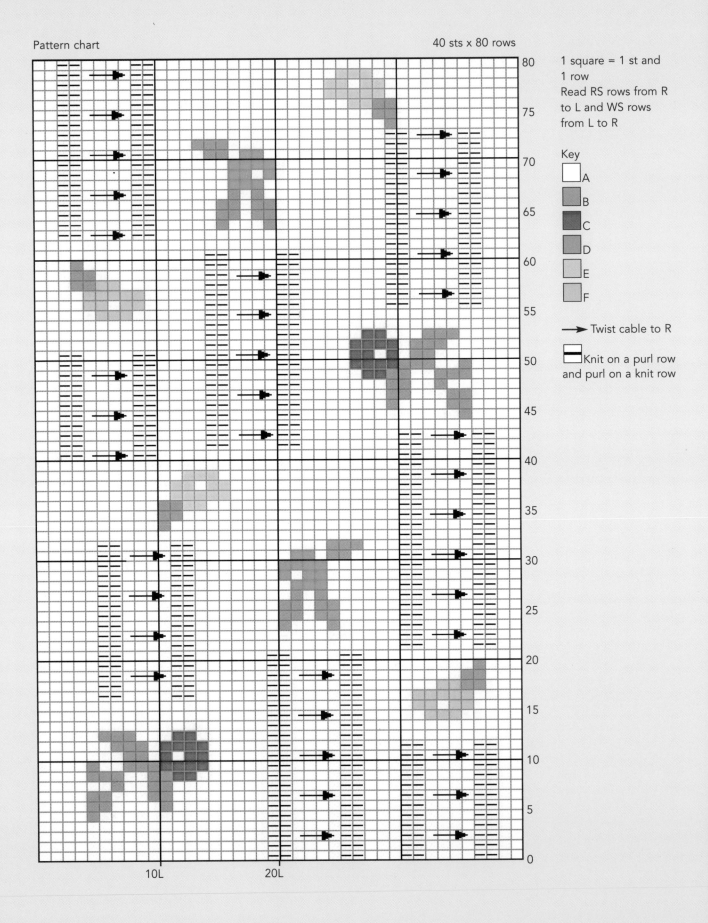

1 square = 1 st and
1 row
Read RS rows from R
to L and WS rows
from L to R

Key

A
B
C
D
E
F

→ Twist cable to R

Knit on a purl row
and purl on a knit row

Main image page 33

Snowberry

Japanese wrapping cloths provided the inspiration for this delicate, understated cardigan with crochet trim. A yoke is suggested by the mirror image at the front and back.

SIZES
To fit 32[34:36:38:40]in
(81[86:91:97:102]cm
See schematic for actual measurements

MATERIALS
Rowan Felted Tweed 191yd (175m)
per 50g ball
7[7:7:8:8] balls colour A:
     Carbon (159)
1[1:1:1:1] ball colour B:
     Ginger (154)
1[1:1:1:1] ball colour C:
     Bilberry (151)
1[1:1:1:1] ball colour D:
     Watery (152)
Rowan RYC Cashsoft DK 142yd
(130m) per 50g ball
1[1:1:1:1] ball colour E:
     Belladonna (502)
1[1:1:1:1] ball colour F:
     Clementine (510)
1[1:1:1:1] ball colour G:
     Lime (509)
Rowan Scottish Tweed 4-ply 120yd
(110m) per 25g ball
* 1[1:1:1:1] ball colour H:
     Lavender (05)
* Use yarn double
Needles: One pair each 3mm (US 2/3)
and 3.75mm (US 5) 3mm (US D3)
Crochet hook

Stitch holders
Buttons: 7 x ½in (1cm)

TENSION
24 sts and 32 rows to 4in (10cm)
measured over st st pattern using
larger needles.

STITCHES USED
Stocking stitch (page 144)
Moss (seed) stitch (page 144)
Crochet techniques (pages 152–3)
Crochet picot edge (page 153)

CROCHET ABBREVIATIONS
Ch = chain; dc = double crochet

Back
Using smaller needles and colour A
Cast on 123[129:135:141:147] sts
Row 1 (RS): K1, *p1, k1, rep from *
to end.
Row 2: As row 1.
These 2 rows form moss st.
Work in moss st for a further 16 rows,
ending with a WS row.
Change to larger needles.
Beg with a knit row, work in st st for
2 rows, ending with a WS row.
Place border chart
Using the **woven intarsia** technique
(see page 148), and starting and ending
rows as indicated work as folls:
Work 12 rows, ending with chart row
12 and a WS row.
Break off all contrasts and cont in st
st, beg with a K row, using yarn A
only as folls:
Cont straight until back measures
11[11½:11½:11¾:11¾]in
(28[29:29:30:30]cm), ending with a
WS row.
Shape armholes
Cast off 6 sts at beg of next 2 rows.
111[117:123:129:135] sts.
Place yoke chart
Using the **woven intarsia** technique and
starting and ending rows as indicated,
cont in patt from chart as folls:
Work 64 rows, ending with a WS row.
Break off all contrasts and cont in st
st, beg with a K row, using yarn A
only as folls:
Cont straight until armhole measures
9[9:9½:9½:10]in [23:23:24:24:25]cm,
ending with a WS row.

Shape shoulders and back neck
Cast off 12[13:14:14:15] sts at beg
of next 2 rows. 87[91:95:101:105] sts.
Next row: (RS) Cast off
12[13:14:14:15] sts,
Work until there are 16[16:17:19:20]
sts on right needle and turn, leaving
rem sts on a holder.
Work each side of neck separately.
Cast off 4 sts at beg of next row.
Cast off rem 12[12:13:15:16] sts.
With RS facing, rejoin yarn to rem sts,
cast off centre 31[33:33:35:35] sts,
knit to end.
Complete to match first side,
reversing shapings.

Left Front
Using smaller needles and colour A
cast on 67[71:73:77:79] sts
Work in moss st as given for back for
17 rows, ending with a RS row.
Row 18: (WS) Moss st 7 sts and slip
these sts onto a holder, m1, moss st
to last 1[0:1:0:1] st, (inc in last st)
1[0:1:0:1] times.
62[65:68:71:74] sts.
Change to larger needles.
Beg with a knit row, work in st st for 2
rows, ending with a WS row.
Place border chart
Starting and ending rows as
indicated, work in patt foll border
chart as folls:
Work 12 rows, ending with chart row
12 and a WS row.
Break off all contrasts and cont in st
st, beg with a knit row, using yarn A
only as folls:
Cont straight until left front matches
back to beg of armhole shaping,
ending with a WS row.
Shape armhole
Cast off 6 sts at beg of next row.
56[59:62:65:68] sts.
Work 1 row, ending with a WS row.
Place yoke chart
Starting and ending rows as
indicated, cont in patt from chart
as folls:
Cont straight until 19[19:19:21:21]
rows less have been worked than on
back to start of shoulder shaping,
ending with a RS row.

Shape neck

Keeping chart correct work until chart row 64 has been completed and then cont using yarn A only, cast off 8[9:9:9:9] sts at beg of next row, then 4 sts at beg of foll alt row.
44[46:49:52:55] sts.
Dec 1 st at neck edge of next 4 rows, then on foll 4[4:4:5:5] alt rows.
36[38:41:43:46] sts.
Work 4 rows, ending with a WS row.

Shape shoulder

Cast off 12[13:14:14:15] sts at beg of next and foll alt row.
Work 1 row.
Cast off rem 12[12:13:15:16] sts.

Right Front

Using smaller needles and colour A cast on 67[71:73:77:79] sts
Work in moss st as given for back for 10 rows, ending with a WS row.
Row 11: (RS) K1, p1, k2tog, yfwd (to make a buttonhole), moss st to end.
Work in moss st for a further 6 rows, ending with a RS row.
Row 18: (WS) (Inc in first st) 1[0:1:0:1] times, moss st to last 7 sts, m1 and turn, leaving last 7 sts on a holder.
62[65:68:71:74] sts.
Change to larger needles and complete to match left front, foll chart for right front and reversing shapings.

Sleeves

Using smaller needles and colour A cast on 53[53:55:57:57] sts
Work in moss st as given for back for 16 rows, ending with a WS row.
Cont in moss st, inc 1 st at each end of next and foll 6th row.
57[57:59:61:61] sts.
Work 1 row, ending with a WS row.
Change to larger needles.
Beg with a knit row, work in st st for 2 rows, ending with a WS row.

Place border chart

Starting and ending rows as indicated, work in patt foll border chart until chart row 12 has been completed and then cont using yarn A only at the same time inc 1 st at each end of 3rd and every foll 6th[6th:6th:6th:4th] row to 69[69:67:73:119] sts, then on every foll 4th[4th:4th:4th:0] row, first four sizes only, until there are 107[107:113:113:119] sts.
Cont straight until sleeve measures 18½[:18½:19:19:19]in (47[47:48:48:48] cm), ending with a WS row. Cast off.

Finishing

Tidy loose ends back into their own colours. Block pieces to correct measurements.
Join shoulder seams.

Button band

Slip 7 sts left on left front holder onto smaller needles and rejoin colour A with RS facing.
Cont in moss st as set until band, when slightly stretched, fits up left front opening edge to neck shaping, ending with a WS row.
Break yarn and leave sts on a holder.
Slip stitch band in position.
Mark positions for 7 buttons on this band – first to come level with buttonhole already worked in right front, last to come ³⁄₈in (1cm) up from neck shaping and rem 5 buttons evenly spaced between.

Buttonhole band

Slip 7 sts left on right front holder onto smaller needles and rejoin colour A with WS facing.
Cont in moss st as set until band, when slightly stretched, fits up right front opening edge to neck shaping, ending with a WS row and with the addition of a further 5 buttonholes worked as folls:

(continued overleaf)

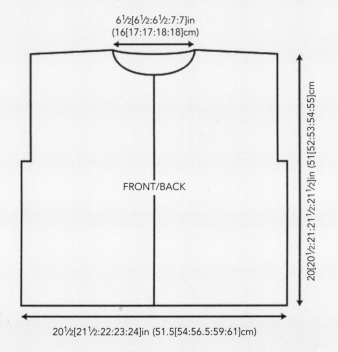

6½[6½:6½:7:7]in
(16[17:17:18:18]cm)

20[20½:21:21½:21½]in (51[52:53:54:55]cm)

FRONT/BACK

20½[21½:22:23:24]in (51.5[54:56.5:59:61]cm)

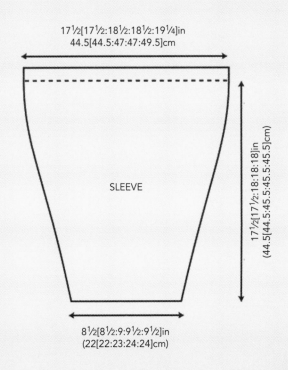

17½[17½:18½:18½:19¼]in
44.5[44.5:47:47:49.5]cm

17½[17½:18:18:18]in
(44.5[44.5:45.5:45.5:45.5]cm)

SLEEVE

8½[8½:9:9½:9½]in
(22[22:23:24:24]cm)

Buttonhole row: (RS) K1, p1, k2tog yfwd (to make a buttonhole), k1, p1, k1.

Do NOT break off yarn.

Slip st band into position.

Neckband

With RS facing, smaller needles and yarn A, moss st across 7 sts of buttonhole band, pick up and knit 31[32:32:34:34] sts up right side of neck, 39[41:41:43:43] sts from front, and 31[32:32:34:34] sts down left side of neck, then moss st across 7 sts of button band.

115[119:119:125:125] sts.

Work in moss st as set by front bands for 3 rows, ending with a WS row.

Row 4: (RS) K1, p1, k2tog, yfwd (to make 7th buttonhole), moss st to end.

Work in moss st for a further 3 rows.

Cast off in moss st.

Set sleeve head into armhole, the straight sides at top of sleeve to form a neat right angle to cast off sts at armhole at back and front.

Sew side seams and sleeve seams.

CROCHET PICOT EDGE

Using crochet hook and colour A and with RS facing rejoin colour A to L front at lower edge of front opening.

Working into sts of cast on edge work picot edge as folls:

1 dc into first st, * 4 ch, 1 dc into same place as last dc, ** 1 dc into each of the next 2 sts. Rep from * to end, ending last rep at **.

In the same way work picot edging around lower edge of sleeves and neckband.

Sew on buttons to correspond with buttonholes.

Steam seams.

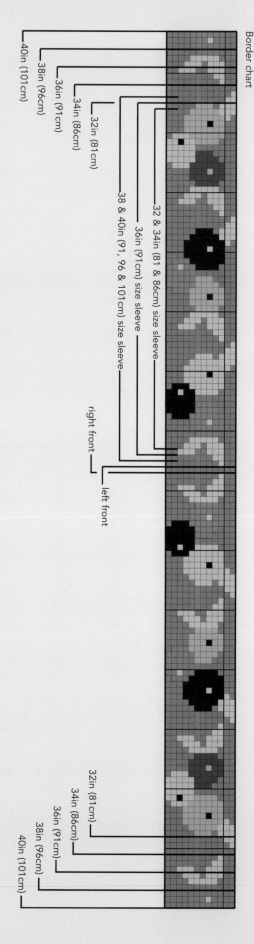

Border chart

40in (101cm)

38in (96cm)

36in (91cm)

34in (86cm)

32in (81cm)

38 & 40in (91, 96 & 101cm) size sleeve

36in (91cm) size sleeve

32 & 34in (81 & 86cm) size sleeve

right front

left front

32in (81cm)

34in (86cm)

36in (91cm)

38in (96cm)

40in (101cm)

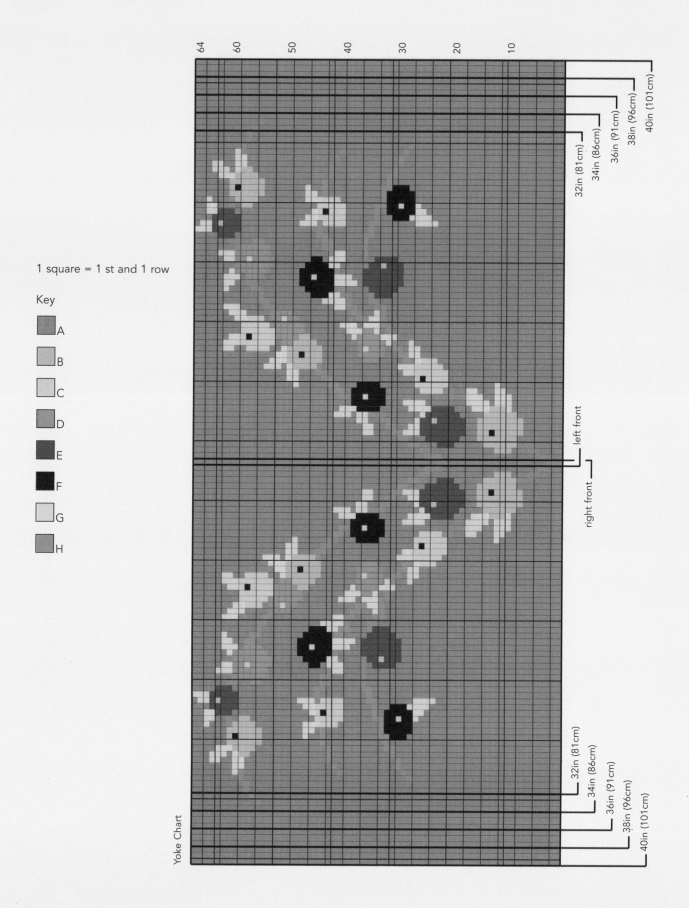

1 square = 1 st and 1 row

Key

A
B
C
D
E
F
G
H

Yoke Chart

64 60 50 40 30 20 10

40in (101cm)
38in (96cm)
36in (91cm)
34in (86cm)
32in (81cm)

left front

right front

32in (81cm)
34in (86cm)
36in (91cm)
38in (96cm)
40in (101cm)

CHAPTER THREE

Tops

Main image page 35

Heath

This early Fair Isle stripe design, updated in 4-ply cotton, is easy to knit. A slightly fitted shape makes a smart cover-up for summer dressing.

SIZES

To fit bust 32[34:37:40:44]in (81[86:94:101:112]cm)
See schematic for actual measurements

MATERIALS

Rowan 4-ply cotton
186yd (170m) per 50g ball
2(2:3:3:4) balls of colour A:
   Bluebell (136)
2(2:3:3:4) balls of colour B:
   Ripple (121)
1(1:1:1:2) balls colour C:
   Ardour (130)
1(1:1:1:2) balls colour D:
   Honeydew (140)
1(1:1:1:2) balls colour E:
   Provence (139)
1(1:1:1:2) balls colour F:
   Aegean (129)
1(1:1:1:2) balls colour G:
   Bleached (113)
Needles: 1 pair each 2.25mm (US 1) and 3mm (US 3)
Stitch holders
Buttons: 7 x ⅜in (1cm)
Ribbon: 2yd (2m), ¼in (0.5cm) wide
Stitch holder

TENSION

26 sts and 35 rows = 4in (10cm) measured over pattern using larger needles.

STITCHES USED

Stocking stitch (page 144)
Moss (seed) stitch (page 144)
2-colour stranded knitting (page 147)

KNITTING NOTES

Work Fair Isle from patt chart. RS rows read R to L (so st 1 is furthest R on first row) starting patt thus:

Back
Commence on st 2[4:1:4:5]
Left Front
Commence on st 2[4:1:4:3]
Right Front
Commence on st 1[3:12:3:2]
Sleeve
Commence on st 6[2:4:5:3]

Back

Using smaller needles and colour A cast on 111[115:121:127:141] sts.
Row 1: (RS) K1, *p1, k1, rep from * to end.
Row 2: As row 1.
These 2 rows form moss st and are rep throughout. Work in moss st for a further 4 rows, ending with RS facing for next row. Change to larger needles and rep the 66 row patt and, using the **2-colour stranded knitting** technique (described on page 147), cont in patt from chart thus:
Work 8 rows, ending with RS facing for next row. Keeping patt correct, dec 1 st each end of next and every foll 6th row until 103[107:113:119:133] sts rem. Work 13 rows, ending with RS facing for next row. Inc 1 st at each end of next and every foll 10th row until there are 115[119:125:131:145] sts, taking inc sts into patt.
Cont straight until back measures 12[12:12:12½:12½]in (30.5[30.5:30.5:31.5:31.5]cm) ending with RS facing for next row.
Shape armholes
Keeping patt correct, cast off 5[5:5:6:6] sts at beg of next 2 rows. Dec 1 st at each end of next 5[5:5:5:6] rows, then on foll 1[2:3:3:6] alt rows, then on every foll 4th row until 91[93:95:97:101] sts. Cont straight until armhole measures 6½[7:7½:8:9]in (17[18.5:19.5:21:23]cm), ending with RS facing for next row.

Shape neck and shoulders

Cast off 8[9:9:9:9] sts at beg off next 2 rows. 75[75:77:79:81] sts.
Next row: (RS) Cast off 8[9:9:9:9] sts, patt until there are 13[12:12:13:14] sts on R needle and turn, leaving rem sts on a holder. Work each side of neck separately.
Cast off 4 sts at beg of next row, work to end. Cast off 8[9:9:9:9] sts at beg of next row, work 1 row. Cast off rem 9[8:8:9:10] sts.
With RS facing, rejoin yarns to rem sts, cast off to last 20[21:21:22:22] sts, patt to end.
Complete to match first side, reversing shapings.

Left Front

Using smaller needles and colour A cast on 61[63:67:71:77] sts. Work in moss st as given for back for 5 rows, ending with WS facing for next row.
Row 6: (WS) Moss st 6 sts and slip these sts onto a holder, moss st to last st and inc in last st, 56[58:62:66:72] sts. Change to larger needles. Cont in patt from chart thus:
Work 8 rows, ending with RS facing for next row. Keeping patt correct, dec 1 st at beg of next and every foll 6th row until 52[54:58:62:68] sts. Work 13 rows, ending with RS facing for next row. Inc 1 st at beg of next and every foll 10th row until 58[60:64:68:74] sts, taking inc sts into patt.
Cont straight until left front matches back to beg of armhole shaping, ending with RS facing for next row.
Shape armhole
Keeping patt correct cast off 5[5:5:6:6] sts at beg of next row. Work 1 row. Dec 1 st at armhole edge on next 5[5:5:5:6] rows, then on foll 1[2:3:3:6] alt rows, then on foll 1[1:2:3:4] 4th rows. At the same time when there are 52[54:58:61:67] sts.
Shape front
Keeping armhole shaping correct as set, dec 1 st at front edge on next and every foll alt row 12[11:11:12:8] times, work 3 rows. Dec 1 st at front edge on next and every foll 3rd row until 25[26:26:27:28] sts rem.

Work straight until L front matches back to beg of shoulder shaping, ending with RS facing for next row.

Shape shoulder

Cast off 8[9:9:9:9] sts at beg of next and foll alt row, work 1 row. Cast off rem 9[8:8:9:10] sts.

Right Front

Using smaller needles and colour A cast on 61[63:67:71:75] sts. Work in moss st as given for back for 5 rows, ending with WS facing for next row.
Row 6: (WS) Inc in first st, moss st to last 6 sts and turn, leaving rem 6 sts on a holder, 56[58:62:66:70] sts. Complete as given for L front reversing all shapings.

Sleeves

Using smaller needles and colour A cast on 83[87:91:93:101] sts. Work in moss st as given for back for 6 rows, ending with RS facing for next row. Change to larger needles. Start at row 17 and cont in patt from chart thus: Inc 1 st at each end of next and every foll 4th row until there are 89[93:97:99:107] sts taking inc sts into patt. Work straight until sleeve measures 2½in (6cm) ending with RS facing for next row.

Shape top

Keeping patt correct, cast off 5[5:5:6:6] sts at beg of next 2 rows. Dec 1 st at each end of next 10[10:10:8:8] rows. Work 1 row. Dec 1 st at each end of next 13[15:17:21:27] alt rows. Dec 1 st at each end of every row until 13 sts rem. Cast off.

Finishing

Tidy loose ends back into their own colours. Block pieces to correct measurements avoiding moss st trims.

Button band

Slip 6 sts from L front holder onto smaller needles and using colour A with RS facing rejoin yarn. Cont in moss st as set until button band, when slightly stretched, fits up L front opening edge, up L front slope and across to centre back neck, ending with RS facing for next row. Cast off in moss st.

Mark positions for 7 buttons on this band – first to come level with chart row 1, last to come just below beg of front slope shaping, and rem 5 buttons evenly spaced between.

Buttonhole band

Slip 6 sts from R front holder onto smaller needles and using colour A with WS facing rejoin yarn. Cont in moss st as set until button band, when slightly stretched, fits up R opening edge, up R front slope and across to centre back neck, ending with RS facing for next row and with the addition of 7 buttonholes worked to correspond with positions marked for buttons as folls:

Buttonhole row: (RS) K1, p2tog, yrn (to make a buttonhole), p1, k1, p1. When band is complete cast off in moss st. Join shoulder seams. Join ends of bands together. Slip st bands in place. Set in sleeves. Join side seams and sleeve seams. Sew on buttons to correspond with buttonholes. Steam seams. Thread ribbon at waistline using picture as guide.

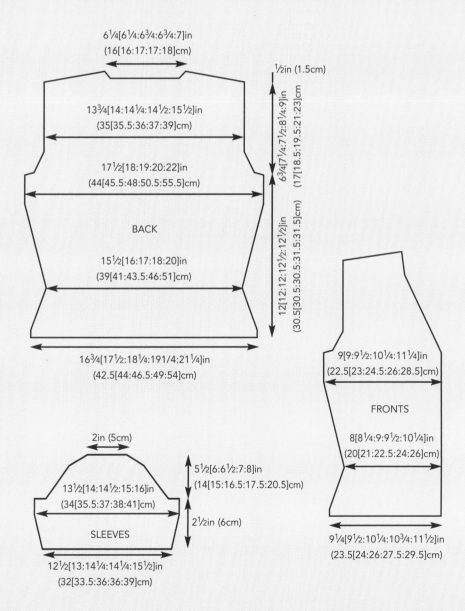

6¼[6¼:6¾:6¾:7]in
(16[16:17:17:18]cm)

½in (1.5cm)

13¾[14:14¼:14½:15½]in
(35[35.5:36:37:39]cm)

6¾[7¼:7½:8¼:9]in
(17[18.5:19.5:21:23]cm)

17½[18:19:20:22]in
(44[45.5:48:50.5:55.5]cm)

BACK

15½[16:17:18:20]in
(39[41:43.5:46:51]cm)

12[12:12:12½:12½]in
(30.5[30.5:30.5:31.5:31.5]cm)

16¾[17½:18¼:19¼:21¼]in
(42.5[44:46.5:49:54]cm)

9[9:9½:10¼:11¼]in
(22.5[23:24.5:26:28.5]cm)

FRONTS

8[8¼:9:9½:10¼]in
(20[21:22.5:24:26]cm)

9¼[9½:10¼:10¾:11½]in
(23.5[24:26:27.5:29.5]cm)

2in (5cm)

13½[14:14½:15:16]in
(34[35.5:37:38:41]cm)

5½[6:6½:7:8]in
(14[15:16.5:17.5:20.5]cm)

2½in (6cm)

SLEEVES

12½[13:14¼:14¼:15½]in
(32[33.5:36:36:39]cm)

Fair Isle chart   12 sts x 66 rows

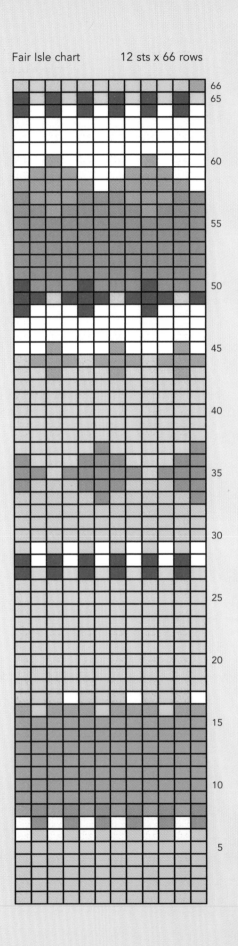

1 square = 1 st and 1 row
Read RS rows from R to L and WS
rows from L to R

Key

□ A
▦ B
▫ C
■ D
▨ E
▩ F
▤ G

Blue colourway main image page 37 *Rust colourway main image page 36*

Aster

Light and airy for summer, a chequer-board pattern is made with alternate blocks of intarsia flowers and Fountain lace.

SIZES
To fit bust 32[34:36:38:40]in
(81[86:91:97:102]cm)
See schematic for actual measurements

MATERIALS
Blue colourway
Rowan 4-ply cotton
186yd (170m) per 50g ball:
5(6:6:6:7) balls colour A:
    Bluebell (136)
1(1:1:1:1) ball colour B:
    Orchid (120)
1(1:1:1:1) ball colour C:
    Bleached (113)
1(1:1:1:1) ball colour D:
    Fresh (131)
1(1:1:1:1) ball colour E:
    Ardour (130)

Rust colourway
Rowan 4-ply cotton
186yd (170m) per 50g ball:
5(6:6:6:7) balls colour A:
    Bloom (132)
1(1:1:1:1) ball colour B:
    Violetta (146)
1(1:1:1:1) ball colour C:
    Mandarine (142)
1(1:1:1:1) ball colour D:
    Bleached (113)
1(1:1:1:1) ball colour E:
    Orchid (120)

Needles: 1 pair each 2.25mm (US 1)
and 3mm (US 2/3)
Stitch holders
Buttons: 7 x ½in (1cm)

TENSION
28 sts and 38 rows to 4in (10cm)
measured over pattern using
larger needles.

STITCHES USED
Stocking stitch (page 144)
Moss (seed) stitch (page 144)
**Lace and intarsia (see charts on
pages 104 and 105)**

Back
Using smaller needles and colour A
cast on 111[117:125:131:139] sts.
Row 1 (RS): K1, *P1, K1, rep from *
to end.
Row 2: As row 1.
These 2 rows form moss st.
Work in moss st for a further 4 rows,
ending with RS facing for next row.
Change to larger needles.
Beg and ending rows as indicated and
repeating the 64 row patt repeat
throughout, using the **woven intarsia**
technique as described on page 148,
cont in patt from chart as folls:
Work 8 rows, ending with RS facing
for next row.
Keeping patt correct, dec 1 st at
each end of next and every foll 6th
row until 103[109:117:123:131] sts rem.
Work 13 rows, ending with RS facing
for next row.

Inc 1 st at each end of next and every
foll 10th row until there are
115[121:129:135:143] sts, taking inc
sts into patt.
Cont straight until back measures
11½[11¾:11¾:12¼:12¼]in
(29[30:30:31:31]cm), ending with RS
facing for next row.
Shape armholes
Keeping patt correct, cast off
5[6:6:7:7] sts at beg of next 2 rows.
105[109:117:121:129] sts.
Dec 1 st at each end of next
5[5:7:7:9] rows, then on foll 1[2:2:3:3]
alt rows, then on foll 4th row.
91[93:97:99:103] sts.
Cont straight until armhole measures
7½[7½:8:8:8¼]in (19[19:20:20:21]cm),
ending with RS facing for next row.
Shape shoulders and back neck
Cast off 8[8:8:8:9] sts at beg of next
2 rows.
75[77:81:83:85] sts.
Next row: (RS) Cast off 8[8:8:8:9] sts,
patt until there are 11[11:13:13:13]
sts on right needle and turn, leaving
rem sts on a holder.
Work each side of neck separately.
Cast off 4 sts at beg of next row.
Cast off rem 7[7:9:9:9] sts.
With RS facing, rejoin yarns to rem
sts, cast off centre 37[39:39:41:41]
sts, patt to end.
Complete to match first side,
reversing shapings.

Left Front
Using smaller needles and colour A
cast on 61[65:69:71:75] sts.
Work in moss st as given for back for
5 rows, ending with WS facing for
next row.
Row 6: (WS) Moss st 6 sts and slip
these sts onto a holder, moss st to
last 1[0:0:1:1] st, (inc in last st)
1[0:0:1:1] times. 56[59:63:66:70] sts.
Change to larger needles.
Beg and ending rows as indicated,
cont in patt from chart as folls:
Work 8 rows, ending with RS facing
for next row.
Keeping patt correct, dec 1 st at beg
of next and every foll 6th row until
52[55:59:62:66] sts rem.
Work 13 rows, ending with RS facing
for next row.

Inc 1 st at beg of next and every foll 10th row until there are 58[61:65:68:72] sts, taking inc sts into patt.
Cont straight until left front matches back to beg of armhole shaping, ending with RS facing for next row.

Shape armhole
Keeping patt correct, cast off 5[6:6:7:7] sts at beg of next row. 53[55:59:61:65] sts.
Work 1 row.
Dec 1 st at armhole edge of next 4 rows, ending with RS facing for next row. 49[51:55:57:61] sts.

Shape front slope
Dec 1 st at armhole edge of next 1[1:3:3:5] rows, then on foll 1[2:2:3:3] alt rows, then on foll 4th row and at same time dec 1 st at front slope edge on next and every foll alt row. 42[42:43:43:44] sts.
Dec 1 st at front slope edge only on 2nd and foll 12[13:10:11:8] alt rows, then on every foll 4th row until 23[23:25:25:27] sts rem.
Cont straight until left front matches back to beg of shoulder shaping, ending with RS facing for next row.

Shape shoulder
Cast off 8[8:8:8:9] sts at beg of next and foll alt row.
Work 1 row. Cast off rem 7[7:9:9:9] sts.

Right Front
Using smaller needles and colour A cast on 61[65:69:71:75] sts.
Work in moss st as given for back for 5 rows, ending with WS facing for next row.
Row 6: (WS) (Inc in first st) 1[0:0:1:1] times, moss st to last 6 sts and turn, leaving rem 6 sts on a holder. 56[59:63:66:70] sts.
Change to larger needles.
Beg and ending rows as indicated, cont in patt from chart as folls:
Work 8 rows, ending with RS facing for next row.
Keeping patt correct, dec 1 st at end of next and every foll 6th row until 52[55:59:62:66] sts rem.
Complete to match left front, reversing shapings, working an extra row before beg of armhole and shoulder shaping.

Sleeves
Using smaller needles and colour A cast on 83[85:89:91:95] sts.
Work in moss st as for back for 6 rows, ending with RS facing for next row.
Change to larger needles.
Beg and ending rows as indicated, cont in patt from chart as folls:
Inc 1 st at each end of next and every foll 4th row until there are 89[91:95:97:101] sts, taking inc sts into patt.
Cont straight until sleeve measures 2in (5cm), ending with RS facing for next row.

Shape top
Keeping patt correct, cast off 5[6:6:7:7] sts at beg of next 2 rows. 79[79:83:83:87] sts.
Dec 1 st at each end of next 5 rows, then on foll 3 alt rows, then on every foll 4th row until 53[53:57:57:61] sts rem.
Work 1 row, ending with RS facing for next row.
Dec 1 st at each end of next and every foll alt row to 43 sts, then on foll 3 rows, ending with RS facing for next row. 37 sts.
Cast off 6 sts at beg of next 4 rows.
Cast off rem 13 sts.

Finishing
Tidy loose ends back into their own colours. Block pieces to correct measurements
Join shoulder seams.
Button band
Slip 6 sts from left front holder onto smaller needles and rejoin yarn A with RS facing.
Cont in moss st as set until button band, when slightly stretched, fits up left front opening edge, up left front slope and across to centre back neck, ending with RS facing for next row.
Cast off in moss st.
Mark positions for 7 buttons on this band – first to come level with chart row 1, last to come just below beg of front slope shaping, and rem 5 buttons evenly spaced between.
Buttonhole band
Slip 6 sts from right front holder onto smaller needles and rejoin yarn A with WS facing.
Cont in moss st as set until button band, when slightly stretched, fits up right front opening edge, up right front slope and across to centre back neck, ending with RS facing for next row and with the addition of 7 button-holes worked to correspond with positions marked for buttons as folls:
Buttonhole row: (RS) K1, P2tog, yrn (to make a buttonhole), P1, K1, P1.
When band is complete, cast off in moss st.
Join ends of bands. Slip stitch bands in place. Set in sleeves.
Join side seams and sleeve seams.
Sew on buttons to correspond with buttonholes.
Steam seams.

13[13:13¼:14:14½]in
(32.5[33:34.5:35.5:36.5]cm)

BACK/FRONT

19[19½:19½:20:20½]in
(48[49:50:51:52]cm)

16[17:18:19:20]in
(41[43:46:48:51]cm)

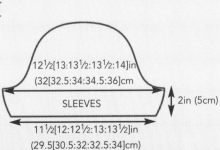

12½[13:13½:13½:14]in
(32[32.5:34:34.5:36]cm)

SLEEVES

2in (5cm)

11½[12:12½:13:13½]in
(29.5[30.5:32:32.5:34]cm)

Pattern chart:

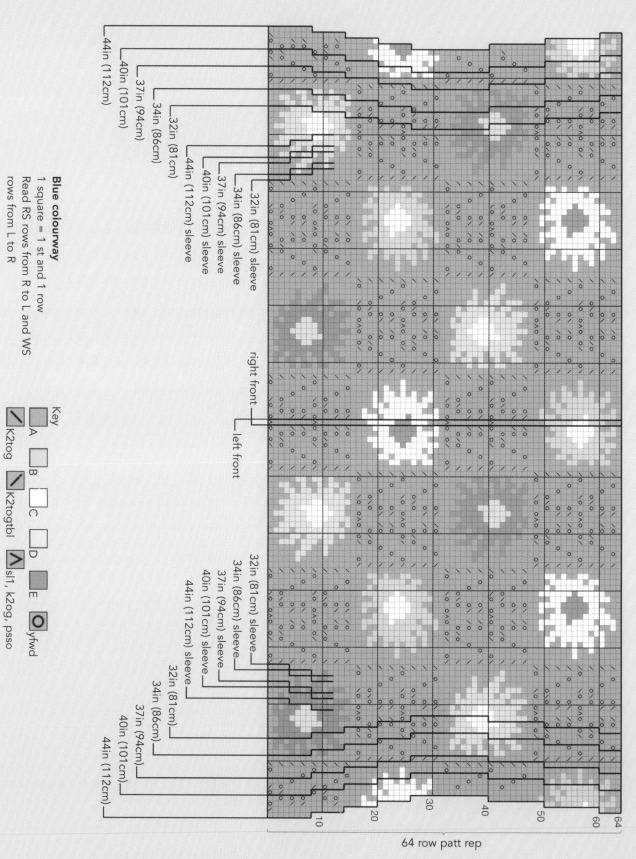

44in (112cm)
40in (101cm)
37in (94cm)
34in (86cm)
32in (81cm)
44in (112cm) sleeve
40in (101cm) sleeve
37in (94cm) sleeve
34in (86cm) sleeve
32in (81cm) sleeve

right front

left front

32in (81cm) sleeve
34in (86cm) sleeve
37in (94cm) sleeve
40in (101cm) sleeve
44in (112cm) sleeve
32in (81cm)
34in (86cm)
37in (94cm)
40in (101cm)
44in (112cm)

Blue colourway
1 square = 1 st and 1 row
Read RS rows from R to L and WS
rows from L to R

Key

A
B
C
D
E

K2tog
K2togtbl
sl1, k2og, psso
yfwd

10
20
30
40
50
60
64

64 row patt rep

Pattern chart:

64 row patt rep

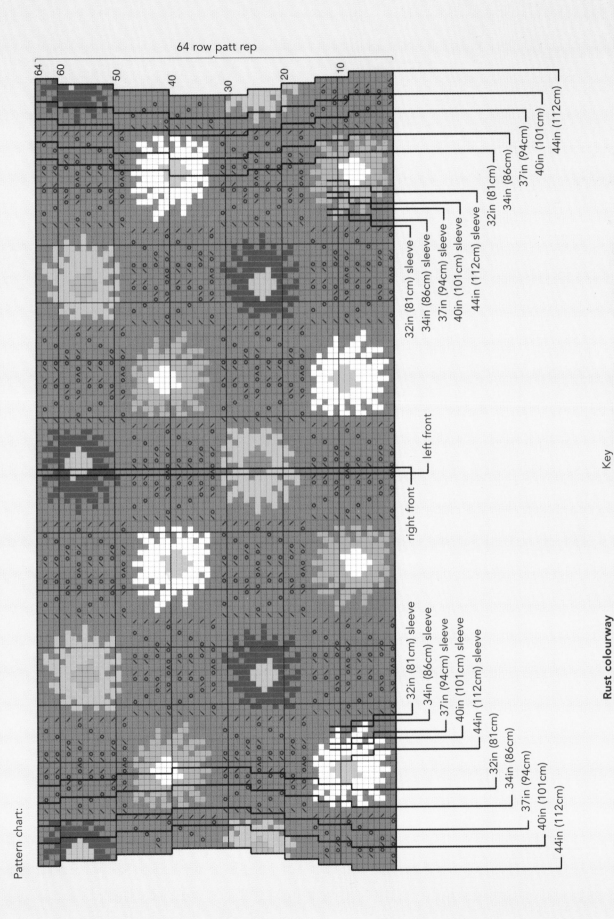

64 60 50 40 30 20 10

32in (81cm) sleeve
34in (86cm) sleeve
37in (94cm) sleeve
40in (101cm) sleeve
44in (112cm) sleeve

32in (81cm)
34in (86cm)
37in (94cm)
40in (101cm)
44in (112cm)

left front

right front

32in (81cm) sleeve
34in (86cm) sleeve
37in (94cm) sleeve
40in (101cm) sleeve
44in (112cm) sleeve

32in (81cm)
34in (86cm)
37in (94cm)
40in (101cm)
44in (112cm)

Key

A B C D E ○ yfwd
╱ K2tog ╱ K2togtbl ◥ sl1, k2og, psso

Rust colourway

1 square = 1 st and 1 row
Read RS rows from R to L and WS
rows from L to R

ASTER 105

Main image page 38

Heartsease

My favourite spring wildflower, the heartsease, is used here together with tiny cables to make a year-round wearable top to pair with jeans or a skirt.

SIZES
To fit bust 32[34:36:38:40]in (81[86:91:96:102]cm)
See schematic for actual measurements

MATERIALS
Jamieson and Smith 4-ply wool 118m (129yd) per 25g ball
6[7:8:9:10] balls colour A:
    Blue Mix (FC15)
1[1:1:1:1] ball colour B:
    Crocus (133)
1[1:1:1:1] ball colour C:
    Pink (1283)
1[1:1:1:1] ball colour D:
    Lilac (49)
1[1:1:1:1] ball colour E:
    Purple (20)
1[1:1:1:1] ball colour F:
    Pale Yellow (66)
1[1:1:1:1] ball colour G:
    Turquoise (65)
Needles: 1 pair each 2.75mm (US 2) and 3.25mm (US 4)
Stitch holders

TENSION
35 sts and 36 rows to 4in (10cm) measured over st st and cable pattern using larger needles. 38 sts and 35 rows to 4in (10cm) measured over 1 x 1 twisted rib using smaller needles.

STITCHES USED
Stocking stitch (page 144)
Cable 4 front (C4F) (page 145)
Cable 4 back (C4B) (page 145)
1 x 1 twisted rib (page 144)

Back
Rib only.
With smaller needles and colour A cast on 146[150:160:170:178] sts.
Work in 1 x 1 twisted rib until piece measures 11[11:11.5:11.5:12]in (28[28:29.5:29.5:31]cm).

Shape armholes
Cast off 11 sts at beg of next 2 rows, 124[128:138:148:156]sts
Dec 1 st at each end of next 13 rows, then on foll 5[5:6:6:8] alt rows, 88[92:100:110:114] sts.
Cont straight until armhole measures 8[8:8½:8½:9]in (20.5[20.5:21.5:21.5:23]cm) ending with RS facing for next row.

Shape back neck and shoulders
Next row: (RS) Rib 16[16:18:19:20] sts and turn, leaving rem sts on a holder.
Work each side of neck separately.
Cast off 4 sts at beg of next row.
Cast off rem 12[12:14:15:16] sts.
With RS facing, rejoin yarn to rem sts.
Cast off centre 56[60:64:72:74] sts knit to end.
Complete to match first side, reversing shapings.

Front
With larger needles and colour A cast on 146[150:160:170:178] sts
Start and work from patt using the **woven intarsia** technique (described on page 148) on chart thus:
Row 1: K0[2:7:12:16] sts, work chart rep 3 times then first 8 sts once more, k0[2:7:12:16] sts.
Row 2: P0[2:7:12:16] sts, work chart rep 3 times then first 8 sts once more, p0[2:7:12:16] sts.
Cont in patt as set with 2nd and foll sides maintaining a st st border either side of patterning at side edges until work measures 11[11:11.5:11.5:12]in (28[28:29.5:29.5:31]cm).

Shape armholes
Cast off 11 sts at beg of next 2 rows, 124[128:138:148:156]sts
Dec 1 st at each end of next 13 rows,

then on foll 5[5:6:6:8] alt rows, 88[92:100:110:114] sts.
Work 7 rows ending with RS facing for next row.

Shape neck
Next row: K29 sts and turn, leaving rem sts on a holder.
Work each side of neck separately
Dec 1 st at neck edge of next 7[8:9:10:10] rows, then on foll 10[10:10:12:12] alt rows, 12[12:14:15:16] sts.
Cont straight until front measures same as back to shoulder, ending with RS facing for next row.

Shape shoulder
Cast off rem 12[12:14:15:16] sts.
With RS facing, rejoin yarn to rem sts, cast off centre 30[32:34:36:38]sts.
Knit to end.
Complete to match first side, reversing shapings.

Neck Border
With smaller needles and colour A cast on 6 sts.
Work cable patt as follows:
Row 1: K4, p2
Row 2: K2, p4
Row 3: C4B, p2
Row 4: P4, k2
Rep row 1 to row 4 until band is long enough when slightly stretched to fit round neck. Cast off.

Armhole Borders (make 2)
With smaller needles and colour A cast on 6 sts.
Work cable patt as for neck border until band is long enough when slightly stretched to fit round armhole. Cast off.

Welt Border
With smaller needles and colour A cast on 6 sts.
Work cable patt as for neck border until band is long enough when slightly stretched to fit across bottom of front. Cast off.

Finishing

Tidy loose ends back into their
own colours. Block pieces to correct
measurements, avoiding cables.
Join shoulder seams.
Pin neckband evenly round neck
with the two purl sts to the sewing
edge and with RS facing sew
band in place.
Armbands and welt band, sew as
for neckband.
Join side seams.
Steam seams.

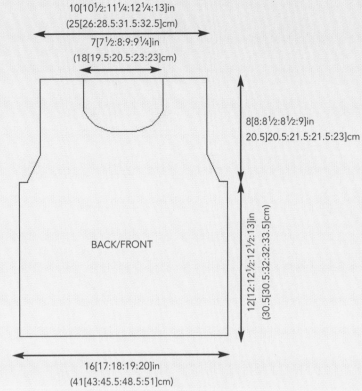

10[10½:11¼:12¼:13]in
(25[26:28.5:31.5:32.5]cm)

7[7½:8:9:9¼]in
(18[19.5:20.5:23:23]cm)

8[8:8½:8½:9]in
20.5]20.5:21.5:21.5:23]cm

BACK/FRONT

12[12:12½:12½:13]in
(30.5[30.5:32:32:33.5]cm)

16[17:18:19:20]in
(41[43:45.5:48.5:51]cm)

Pattern chart: Intarsia, rib and cable

46sts x 32 rows

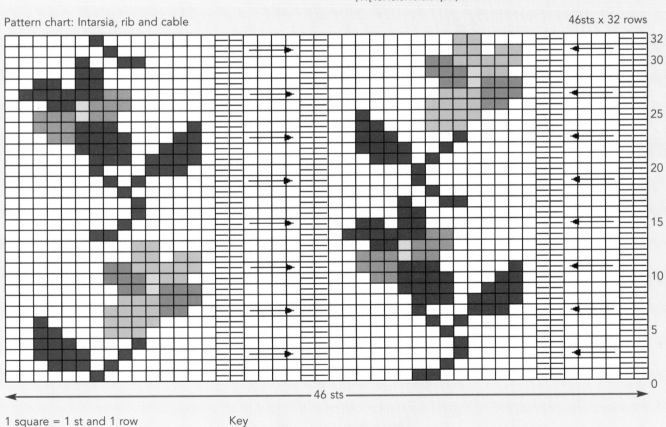

46 sts

1 square = 1 st and 1 row
Read RS rows from R to L and WS
rows from L to R

Key

A B C D E F

G   Purl on knit row and knit on purl row

C4F   C4B

Main image page 40

Liberty Floral

Dressed in Tana lawn smocked frocks from an early age, flower prints from this most famous textile house are in my blood. This fine-tuned cotton camisole is ideal for hot sunny days.

SIZES

To fit bust 32[34:35]in (81[86:89]cm)
See schematic for actual measurements

MATERIALS

Brown Sheep Yarn Company
cotton fine
222yd (203m) per 50g ball
1[1:1] ball in colour A:
    White (100)
3[4:5] balls in colour B:
    Pale Pink (660)
1[1:1] ball in colour C:
    Medium Lilac (800)
1[1:1] ball in colour D:
    Pale Lilac (695)
1[1:1] ball in colour E:
    Green (380)
1[1:1] ball in colour F:
    Navy (550)
1[1:1] ball in colour G:
    Rose (220)
Needles: 1 pair each 2.25mm (US 1)
and 2.75mm (US 2)
Two 2.5mm (US 2) circular needles
40in (102cm) long
Buttons: 5 x $\frac{3}{8}$in (1cm)
Stitch holders

TENSION

35 sts and 38 rows = 4in (10cm) measured over intarsia pattern using larger needles.

STITCHES USED

Stocking stitch (page 144)
Frill (US ruffle) (below)
Double frill (US double ruffle) (below)
1 x 1 twisted rib (page 144)
Twisted cord (page 151)

Back

Lower frill (ruffle)

Using larger needles and colour A, cast on 581[597:621] sts (this is 4 times the number of sts minus 3 that will later be worked in the back).
Row 1: (RS) K1, * k2, with tip of LH needle, slip first st over 2nd st on RH needle; rep from * to end.
Row 2: P1, * p2 tog; rep from * to end – 146[150:156] sts.
Rows 3, 5 and 7: Knit.
Rows 4, 6 and 8: Purl.
Sl sts onto a spare needle.

Top frill (ruffle)

Using smaller needles and colour B, work as for lower frill through row 4 only.
Join frills (double frill, double ruffles)
Next row: (RS) Holding the 2 frills together, with top frill over lower frill, using colour B, k1 st from colour B frill tog with 1 st from colour A frill. Purl 1 row.
Beg Chart Pattern
Row 1: (RS) Using the **woven intarsia** technique (described on page 148) and colour B, K0[0:3], beg with st 3[1:1] L of chart, work 30 – st rep a total of 5 times, end with st 28[30:30], with B, k0[0:3]. Cont to follow chart in this way, rep rows 1 – 32 twice. Piece measures approx 7¾in (19.5cm) from beg.
Drawstring row: (RS) Using colour K1, * yo, k2 tog; rep from * to end. Purl 1 row. Then beg with row 3 of chart, cont to follow chart through row 32. Piece measures approx. 11¾in (28.5 cm) from beg.
Armhole shaping
Cont patt, cast off 8 sts at beg of next 2 rows, cast off 2 sts at beg of next 12[14:16] rows – 106[106:108] sts.

Neck and shoulder straps

Next row: (RS) K8 sts and slip these onto a holder for shoulder strap, cast off 90[90:92] sts for back neck, knit rem 8 sts for other shoulder strap, work in st st only on these 8 sts for 5in (12.5cm).
Cast off. Work other shoulder strap in same way.

Left Front

Using larger needles and colour A, cast on 289[297:309] sts.
Work lower frill in colour A and top frill in colour B and join as on back – 73[75:78] sts. Purl 1 row.
Row 1: (RS) Using colour B, K0[0:3], beg with st 3[1:1] of chart, work 30 st rep a total of 3 times, end last rep with st 15.
Work as for back to drawstring row. Work drawstring row as on back. Then cont in chart patt until same length as back.
Armhole shaping
From armhole edge, cast off 8 sts once, 2 sts 6[7:8] times – 53[53:54] sts.
Neck and shoulder strap
Next row: (RS) K8 sts and slip these onto a holder for shoulder strap, cast off 45[45:46] sts for neck.
Return to 8 strap sts and work in st st only for 5in (12.5cm).
Cast off.

Right Front

Work as for L front, reversing placement of chart patt by beginning with st 16 and reversing neck and shoulder placement.

Finishing

Tidy loose ends back into their own colours. Block pieces to correct measurements.
Left front band
Using smaller needles and colour B, pick up and k 1 st from every row along L front from neck edge to end of lower frill.
Row 1: (WS) * K1 tbl, P1; rep from * to end.
Row 2: Rep row 1. Rep these rows once more.

Cast off in rib. Place markers for 5 buttons ¾in (2cm) from neck edge and space others at 1½in (4cm) intervals.

Right front band

Work as for L front band, making 5 buttonholes opposite markers by yo, K2 tog on row 2 of rib.

Right armhole frill

Using larger needles and colour B, cast on 357 sts.

Work as for lower frill, rows 1–4 on 90 sts. Sl sts onto a spare needle. To join frill to strap edge (that is the edge above the shaped armhole) with smaller needles and B, pick up and k 90 sts from strap edge.

Join armhole frill

With WS of pieces tog, so that frill st st shows on RS, K1 st from frill tog with 1 st from strap edge then cast off while joining frill in this way.

Left armhole frill

Work as for R armhole frill. Join side seams.

Armhole ribbed band

Using smaller needles and colour B, working from RS along the shaped armhole edge and beg and end at joined frill pick up and K45[47:49] sts round armhole edge, work in 1 x 1 twisted rib (as for L front band) for 4 rows.

Cast off in rib. Work other armhole band in same way.

Sew tog armhole bands to side edges of frill.

Frill neck trim

Using larger circular needles and colour B cast on 1,437[1,437:1,453] sts for frill edge.

Work rows 1–4 of lower back frill – 360[360:364] sts.

Leave sts on needle. With other larger circular needle, pick up and k45[45:46] sts from right front neck edge, 90 sts from strap edge, 90[90:92] sts from back neck, 90 sts from strap edge, 45[45:46] sts from left front neck edge – 360[360:364] sts.

Join frill as for armhole frill trim.

Join side seams. With 2 strands of colour A make a 70in (178cm) twisted cord. Knot ends, pull through drawstring row. Sew on buttons to correspond with buttonholes.

Steam seams.

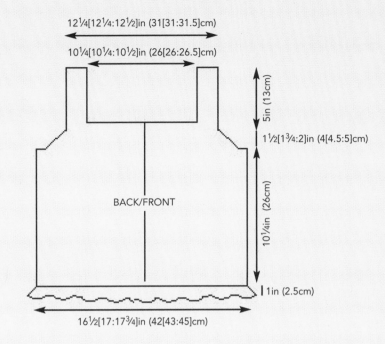

12¼[12¼:12½]in (31[31:31.5]cm)

10¼[10¼:10½]in (26[26:26.5]cm)

5in (13cm)

1½[1¾:2]in (4[4.5:5]cm)

10¼in (26cm)

BACK/FRONT

1in (2.5cm)

16½[17:17¾]in (42[43:45]cm)

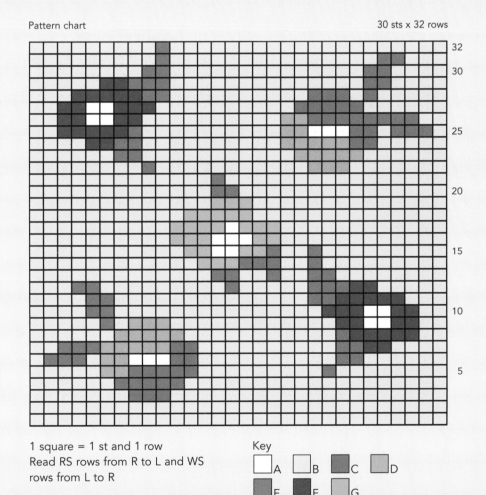

Pattern chart   30 sts x 32 rows

1 square = 1 st and 1 row
Read RS rows from R to L and WS rows from L to R

Key

[ ] A [ ] B [ ] C [ ] D
[ ] E [ ] F [ ] G

CHAPTER FOUR

Jackets & Coats

Coffee colourway main image page 45

Green colourway main image on page 44

Cable Flower

A 1940s-inspired, fitted zip jacket is the foil for a signature cable-and-flower design. An elegant jacket, offering a 'pulled together' vintage look that will never date.

SIZES

To fit bust 32[34:36:40]in
(81[86:91.5:101]cm)
See schematic for actual measurements

MATERIALS

Coffee colourway

Rowan wool/cotton
123yd (113m) per 50g ball
10(11:12:13) balls colour A:
    Coffee Rich (956)
1(1:1:1) ball colour B:
    Hiss (952)
1(1:1:1) ball colour C:
    Tender (951)
1(1:1:1) ball colour D:
    Violet (933)
1(1:1:1) ball colour E:
    Grand (954)
1(1:1:1) ball colour F:
    Bilberry Fool (959)
Rowan Scottish Tweed DK
120yd (110m) per 50g ball
1(1:1:1) ball colour G:
    Lavender (05)

Green colourway

123yd (113m) per 50g ball
10(11:12:13) balls colour A:
    Riviera (930)
1(1:1:1) ball colour B:
    Citron (901)
1(1:1:1) ball colour C:
    Tender (951)
1(1:1:1) ball colour D:
    Hiss (952)
1(1:1:1) ball colour E:
    Antique (900)
1(1:1:1) ball colour F:
    Grand (954)
Rowan Scottish Tweed DK
120yd (110m) per 50g ball
1(1:1:1) ball colour G:
    Lavender (05)
Needles: 1 pair each 3.25 (US 4) and
4mm (US 6)
Open-ended zip to fit
Stitch holder

TENSION

28 sts and 30 rows = 4in (10cm) over intarsia and cable pattern using large needles when relaxed.

STITCHES USED

Stocking stitch (page 144)
1 x 1 twisted rib (page 144)
Cable 4 front (C4F) (page 145)
Cable 4 back (C4B) (page 145)
Bobble (page 146)

Back

Using smaller needles and colour A cast on 112[126:138:150] sts. Work 1in (2.5cm) k1,p1 twisted rib. Change to larger needles and work in patt from chart* using the **woven intarsia** technique (described on page 148), and at the same time shape sides by dec 1 st at each end of 5th and every foll 6th row until 104[118:130:142] sts rem. Work 15 rows ending with a WS row. Inc 1 st at each end of next and every foll 12th row until 112[126:138:150] sts, taking inc sts into pattern. Continue straight until back measures 13¾in (35cm) ending with a WS row.

Shape armholes

Cast off 5[5:5:6] sts at beg of next 2 rows. 102[116:128:138] sts.

3rd and 4th size only: Cast off 3 sts at beg of next 2 rows. 122[132] sts.

All sizes: Dec 1 st at each end of next 7[7:8:9] rows, work 1 row. Dec 1 st at each end of next and every foll alt row 1[4:5:5] times in all, work 3 rows. Dec 1 st at each end of next and every foll 4th row 1[3:3:4] times in all. 84[88:90:96]sts. Work straight until armhole measures 8 [8:8¼:8¼]in (20[20:21:21]cm).

Shape shoulders

Cast off 9 sts at beg of next 2[4:4:4] rows. Cast off 8[8:8:10] sts at beg of next 4[2:2:2] rows. Cast off rem 34[36:38:40] sts.

Left Front

Using smaller needles and colour A cast on 56[63:69:75] sts. Work as given for back to *. Dec 1 st at side edge on 5th and every foll 6th row until 52[59:65:71] sts rem. Work 15 rows ending with a WS row. Inc 1 st at side edge of next and every foll 12th row until there are 56[63:69:75] sts, taking inc sts into pattern. Work straight until front matches back to beg of armhole shaping, ending with a WS row. (Work 1 extra row for R front.)

Shape armhole

Cast off 5[5:5:6] sts at beg of next row, work 1 row 51[55:64:69] sts.

3rd and 4th size only: Cast off 3 sts at beg of next row. Work 1 row. 61[66] sts.

All sizes: Dec 1 st at armhole edge on next 7[7:8:9] rows, work 1 row. Dec 1 st at armhole edge on next and every foll alt row 1[4:5:5] times in all, work 3 rows. Dec 1 st at armhole edge on next and every foll 4th row 1[3:3:4] times in all. 42[44:45:48] sts. Work straight until 15 rows less than on back have been worked to start of shoulder shaping ending with a RS row. (Work 1 extra row for R front.)

Shape neck

Cast off 8[8:9:9] sts at beg of next row, work 1 row. Cast off 3[4:4:5] sts at beg of next row, work 1 row. Dec 1 st at neck edge on next 3 rows. Dec 1 st at neck edge on next and every foll alt row 3 times in all. 25[26:26:28] sts. Work straight until front measures same as back to shoulder ending with a WS row.

Shape shoulder

Cast off 9 sts at beg of next and every foll alt row 1[2:2:2] times in all, work 1 row. Cast off 8[8:8:10] sts at beg of next and every foll alt row 2[1:1:1] times in all.

Right Front

Work as for L front reversing all shaping.

Sleeves

Using smaller needles and colour A cast on 84 sts. Work 3in (7.5cm) k1, p1 twisted rib.

Change to larger needles and follow chart, beg one sleeve on row 1 and second sleeve on row 29. Work 20 rows. Inc 1 st at each end of next and every foll 20th row 0[1:3:4] times in all. 84[86:90:92] sts. Work straight until sleeve measures 17¾ [17¾:19:19]in (45.5[45.5:48:48]cm) from cast on edge, ending with a WS row.

Shape top

Cast off 5 st at beg of next 2 rows. Dec 1 st at each end of next 7[7:10:10] rows. Work 3 rows. Dec 1 st at each end of next and every foll 4th row 9 times. Work 1[1:0:0] rows. Cast off 5 sts at beg of next 4[2:4:2] rows. Cast off 0[6:0:6] sts at beg of next 0[2:0:2] rows. Cast off rem 22 sts.

Finishing

Tidy loose ends back into their own colours.

Front bands

Using smaller needles and colour A, with RS facing, pick up and k1 st for each row from neck shaping to welt. Work 3 rows k1, p1 twisted rib cast off in rib.

Neckband

Join shoulder seams.

Using smaller needles and colour A, with RS facing, pick up and k1 st for each st or row across R front band, up side of neck to R shoulder, across back neck, down L side of neck to end of L front band. Work 2in (5cm) in k1, p1 twisted rib cast off in rib. Sew in sleeves easing fullness at sleeve head into top of armhole. Join side and sleeve seams. Sew in zip.

Zip tag embellishment: Cut 2 x 8in (20.5cm) lengths of each colour G, B, and F. Thread through zip tag top. Make a plait and knot at end. Steam seams.

Measurements based on slightly stretched (sideways) pieces

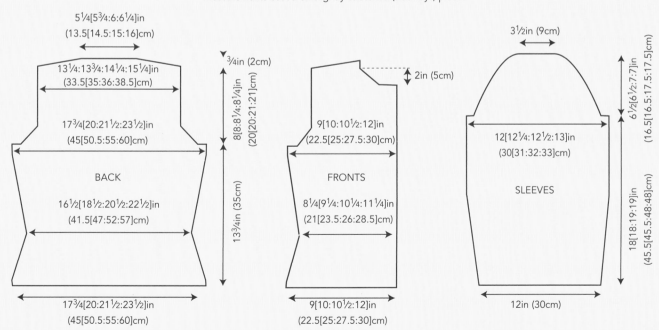

5¼[5¾:6:6¼]in (13.5[14.5:15:16]cm)

13¼[13¾:14¼:15¼]in (33.5[35:36:38.5]cm)

17¾[20:21½:23½]in (45[50.5:55:60]cm)

BACK

16½[18½:20½:22½]in (41.5[47:52:57]cm)

17¾[20:21½:23½]in (45[50.5:55:60]cm)

¾in (2cm)

8[8¼:8¼]in (20[20:21:21]cm)

13¾in (35cm)

2in (5cm)

9[10:10½:12]in (22.5[25:27.5:30]cm)

FRONTS

8¼[9¼:10¼:11¼]in (21[23.5:26:28.5]cm)

9[10:10½:12]in (22.5[25:27.5:30]cm)

3½in (9cm)

6½[6½:7:7]in (16.5[16.5:17.5:17.5]cm)

12[12¼:12½:13]in (30[31:32:33]cm)

SLEEVES

18[18:19:19]in (45.5[45.5:48:48]cm)

12in (30cm)

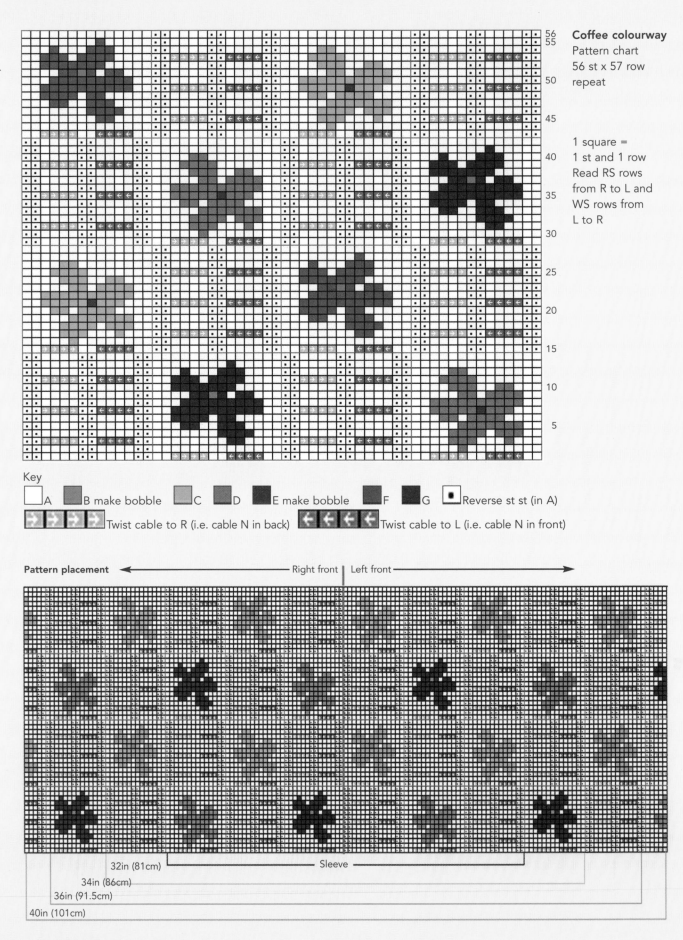

Coffee colourway
Pattern chart
56 st x 57 row
repeat

1 square =
1 st and 1 row
Read RS rows
from R to L and
WS rows from
L to R

56
55

50

45

40

35

30

25

20

15

10

5

Key

A   B make bobble   C   D   E make bobble   F   G   Reverse st st (in A)

Twist cable to R (i.e. cable N in back)   Twist cable to L (i.e. cable N in front)

Pattern placement   ← Right front | Left front →

Sleeve

32in (81cm)
34in (86cm)
36in (91.5cm)
40in (101cm)

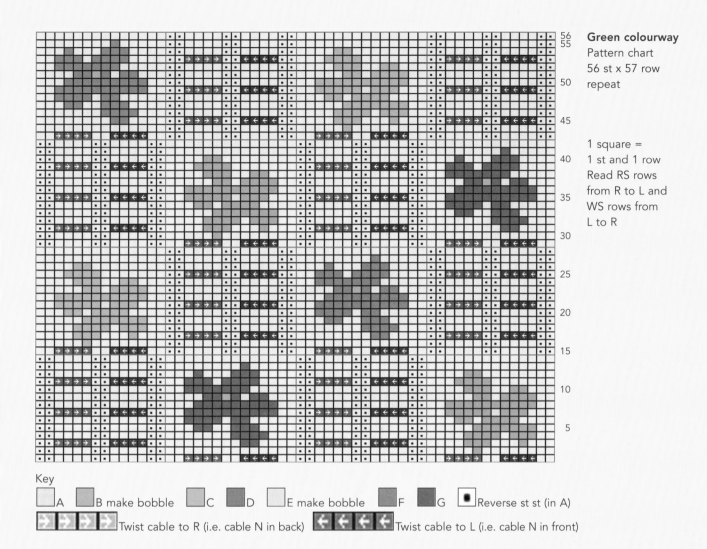

Green colourway
Pattern chart
56 st x 57 row
repeat

1 square =
1 st and 1 row
Read RS rows
from R to L and
WS rows from
L to R

Key

☐ A ■ B make bobble ■ C ■ D ☐ E make bobble ■ F ■ G ▪ Reverse st st (in A)

→ → → → Twist cable to R (i.e. cable N in back) ← ← ← ← Twist cable to L (i.e. cable N in front)

Main image page 47

Harlequin

Inspired by Japanese maple trees, the yoke of this long-line coat cascades into geometric leaf patterns. The garter-stitch trims pick out the leaf colours of this winter-wardrobe staple.

SIZES

To fit bust 32[36:40:44]in (81[91:101:112]cm)
See schematic for actual measurements

MATERIALS

Rowan Scottish Tweed DK 123yd (113m) per 50g ball
12[12:13:14] balls colour A:
    Midnight (23)
1[1:1:1] ball colour B:
    Lobster (17)
1[1:1:1] ball colour C:
    Purple Heather (30)
Rowan Scottish Tweed 4-ply 120yd (110m) per 25g ball
*2[2:2:2] balls colour D:
    Rust (09)
*1[1:2:2] balls colour E:
    Machair (02)
*2[2:2:2] balls colour F:
    Mallard (20)
*1[1:1:1] ball colour G:
    Peat (19)
Rowan Felted Tweed 191yd (175m) per 50g ball
2[2:2:2] balls colour H:
    Melody (142)
Rowan Kid Classic 153 yds (140m) per 50g ball

1[1:1:1] ball colour J:
    Royal (835)
*Use yarn double stranded
Needles: 1 pair each 3.25mm (US3) and 4mm (US6) needles
Buttons: 7 x 1in (2.5cm)

TENSION

21 sts and 29 rows = 4in (10cm) using larger needles over intarsia pattern after light steaming.

STITCHES USED

Stocking stitch (page 144)
Garter stitch (page 144)

Back

Using smaller needles and J cast on 98[110:120:130] sts, and knit 1 row. Work in garter st (knit every row) in stripes thus:
D, knit 2 rows. F, knit 2 rows. B, knit 2 rows**.
Change to larger needles and follow chart A, using the **woven intarsia** technique described on page 148 (and consulting placement guide chart to centralize pattern) from bottom to top 5 times (190 rows)*. Now follow chart B once (68 rows).

Shape shoulders

Using A (background yarn) cast off 10[11:13:14] sts at beg of next 6[2:6:2] rows. Cast off 0[12:0:15] sts at beg of next 0[4:0:4] rows. Cast off rem 38[40:42:42] sts (work measures approx. 41in (104cm) from cast on edge).

Left Front

Using smaller needles and colour J cast on 49[55:60:65] sts. Work as given for back to * but following chart A from centre to edge – as shown in placement guide. Follow appropriate half of chart B to end of row 61.

Shape neck

With RS facing cast off 8[:8:10:10] sts at beg of next row, work 1 row. Cast off 3 sts at beg of next row. Dec 1 st at neck edge on every row until 30[35:39:39] sts rem. Complete chart B patterning so front measures same as back to start of shoulder shaping ending at shoulder edge.

Shape shoulders

Using A cast off 10[11:13:14] sts at beg of next and every foll alt row 3[1:3:1] times in all, work 0[1:0:1]row. Cast off 0[12:0:15] sts at beg of next and every foll alt row 0[2:0:2] times in all.

Right Front

Work as given for L front foll the other half of charts A and B and start neck shaping on row 61.

Sleeves

Using smaller needles and colour J cast on 56[56:60:60] sts. Work as given for back to **. Using J, knit 2 rows and then rep stripe sequence once more.
Change to larger needles and foll chart A (centring patt as pattern placement chart) from bottom to top 3 times (114 rows) at the same time inc 1 st at each end of first and every foll 4th row until 100[102:106:108]sts. Using A cont in st st until sleeve measures 19¼in (49cm) from beg and cast off.

Front Bands

Left band

Using smaller needles and colour B pick up 3 sts from every 4 rows from neck to welt (approx 195 sts). K1 row. Using F, knit 2 rows, using D, knit 2 rows, using J knit 1 row Cast off using J.

Right band

Pick up sts from welt to neck and work as given for L band making 7 buttonholes in the centre of the band, the first ½in (1.5cm) down from neck, the last 10in (25.5cm) up from welt, the rest equally spaced in between. Cast off 3 sts for each buttonhole.

Neckband

Join shoulder seams.
Using smaller needles and B pick up and k1 st for each st or row around the neck including the front bands (approx. 94[96:100:100] sts). Knit 1 row. ***Knit 2 rows F, 2 rows D, 2 rows J, 2 rows B. Rep from *** once more and cast off.

Finishing

Tidy loose ends back into their own colours. Block pieces to correct measurements. With centre of sleeve top at shoulder seam, set in sleeve. Join side and sleeve seams. Sew on buttons to correspond with buttonholes.
Steam seams.

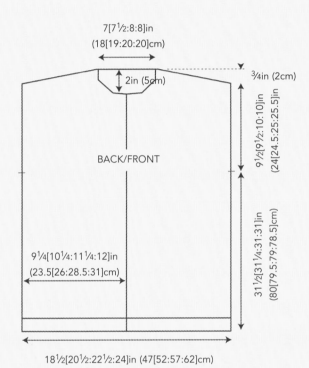

7[7½:8:8]in
(18[19:20:20]cm)

2in (5cm)

¾in (2cm)

9½[9½:10:10]in
(24[24.5:25:25.5]in

BACK/FRONT

31½[31¼:31:31]in
(80[79.5:79:78.5]cm)

9¼[10¼:11¼:12]in
(23.5[26:28.5:31]cm)

18½[20½:22½:24]in (47[52:57:62]cm)

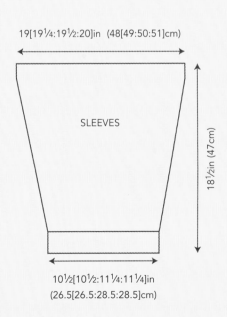

19[19¼:19½:20]in (48[49:50:51]cm)

SLEEVES

18½in (47cm)

10½[10½:11¼:11¼]in
(26.5[26.5:28.5:28.5]cm)

Pattern chart A   60 sts x 38 rows

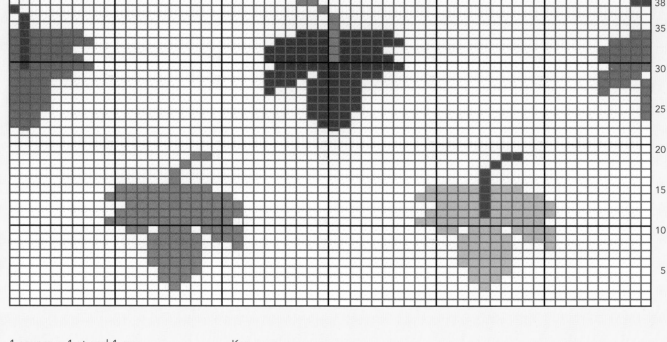

1 square = 1 st and 1 row
Read RS rows from R to L and WS
rows from L to R

Key

◻A ◼B ◼C ◼D ◼E ◼F ◼G ◻H ◼J

Pattern placement

Right front

Left front

Repeat

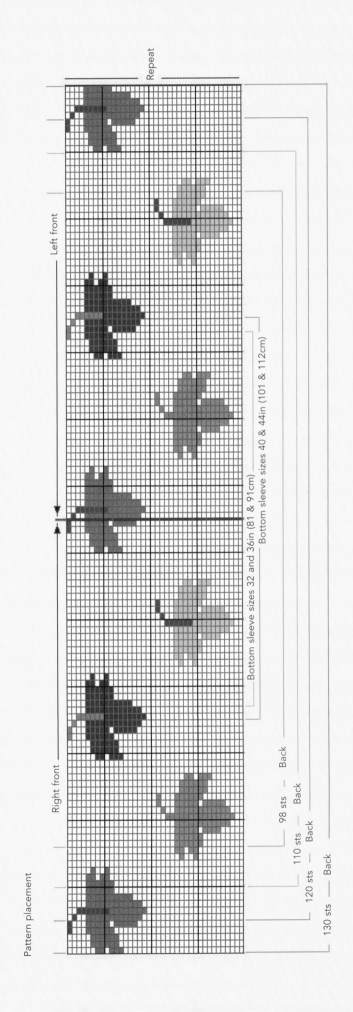

Bottom sleeve sizes 32 and 36in (81 & 91cm)

Bottom sleeve sizes 40 & 44in (101 & 112cm)

98 sts — Back

110 sts — Back

120 sts — Back

130 sts — Back

1 square = 1 st and 1 row
Read RS rows from R to L and WS
rows from L to R

Key

A ☐
B ■
C ■
D ■
E ■
F ■
G ■
H ☐
J ■

Pattern chart B

Notes: Chart is divided into two halves to fit on the pages. For back, work
across both halves of the chart. For fronts, use left front or right front chart.
For size 44in (112cm) + 5 background sts at each edge

60 sts x 68 rows

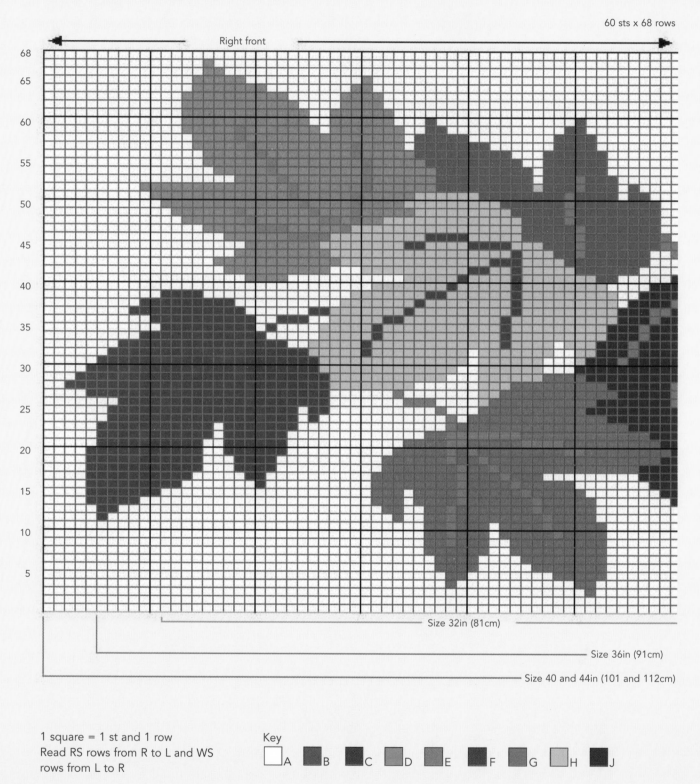

Right front

Size 32in (81cm)

Size 36in (91cm)

Size 40 and 44in (101 and 112cm)

1 square = 1 st and 1 row
Read RS rows from R to L and WS
rows from L to R

Key

A B C D E F G H J

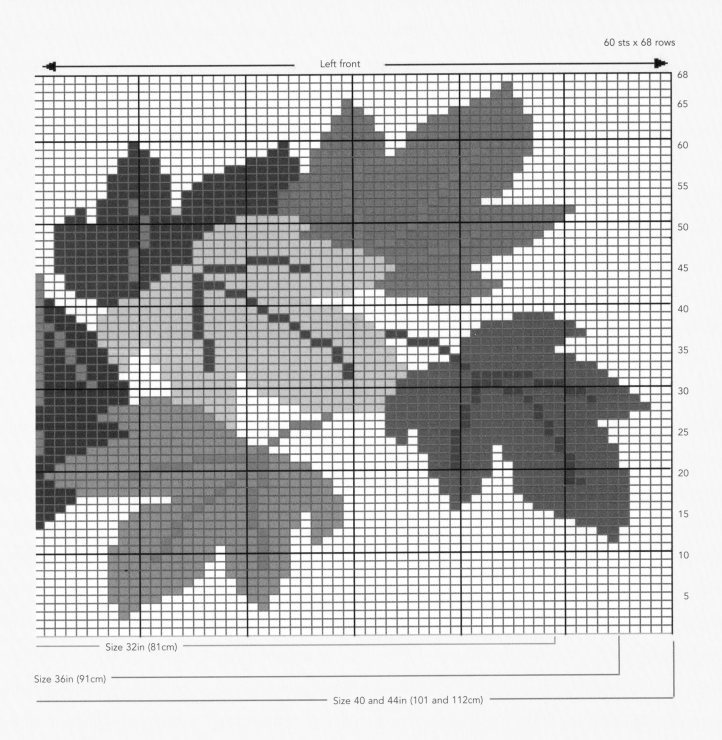

Left front

68
65
60
55
50
45
40
35
30
25
20
15
10
5

Size 32in (81cm)

Size 36in (91cm)

Size 40 and 44in (101 and 112cm)

Main image page 49

Caliope

An exhibition at the Victoria & Albert Museum, in London, UK, sparked off my homage to Ossie Clarke and Celia Birtwell. The long waistcoat body is an excellent canvas for this 1960s-inspired design.

SIZES
To fit bust 36[38:44:]in (91[97:111]cm)
See schematic for actual measurements

MATERIALS
Rowan Summer Tweed
118yd (108m) per 50g hank
13(14:15) hanks colour A:
    Blueberry 525
3(4:4) hanks colour B:
    Cape 511
1(1:1) hanks colour C:
    Sunset 509
1(1:1) hanks colour D:
    Vanity 539
1(1:1) hanks colour E:
    Blossom 541
1(1:1) hanks colour F:
    Summer Berry 537
1(1:1) hanks colour G:
    Angel 526
1(1:1) hanks colour H:
    Butterball 538
1(1:1) hanks colour I:
    Dew 513
Needles: 1 pair each 3.25mm (US 4) and 3.75mm (US 5) needles
One extra long 3.25mm (US 4) circular needle

TENSION
21 sts and 29 rows = 4in (10cm) using larger needles over st st intarsia pattern.

STITCHES USED
Stocking stitch (page144)
Bobble (page 146)
Twisted cord (page 151)
Zigzag border edging (see below)

KNITTING NOTES
To keep pattern chart centred, you may find it helpful to place a yarn marker on the first and last st of pattern – i.e. thus framing the 60 sts – every 30 rows or so.

Make bobble
Row 1: (K1, p1, k1) into next st, turn.
Row 2: K3, turn.
Row 3: P3, turn.
Row 4: K3tog.

Zigzag border edging
Using smaller needles and B cast on 2 sts.
Row 1: Knit.
Row 2: yo, k2.
Row 3: yo, k3.
Row 4: yo, k4.
Row 5: yo, k5.
Row 6: yo, k6.
Row 7: yo, k7.
Row 8: yo, k8.
Row 9: yo, k9 10 sts.
Break off yarn and leave sts on needle. On the same needle, cast on 2 sts and work another point as before. Continue until you have the required number of points. On the last point do not break yarn but turn and knit across all points on the needle.

Half points
Half points are required for some of the sizes, work thus:
Using smaller needles and B cast on 2 sts.
Right front half point border edging
Row 1 and foll alt rows: Knit
Row 2: yo, k2.
Row 4: yo, k3.
Row 6: yo, k4.
Rows 7, 8 and 9: Knit the 5 sts.

Left front half point border edging
Knit 1 row.
Row 2 and foll alt rows: Knit.
Row 3: yo, k2.
Row 5: yo, k3.
Row 7: yo, k4.
Rows 8 and 9: Knit the 5 sts.

Back
Using smaller needles and B work 15[16:17] points. 150[160:170] sts.
Knit 2 rows.
Change to larger needles and A. Start and work from intarsia chart using **woven intarsia** technique decribed on page 148, working 3 rows of st st (commencing with a knit row)* and setting pattern at centre back on 4th row thus:
Work 45[50:55] sts A, work 60 sts from chart, work 45[50:55] sts A. Work in pattern as set throughout.
On 11th row dec 1 st at each end of next and every foll 10th row until 98[108:118] sts. Work straight until back measures 40in (102cm) above points ending with WS row.
Shape armholes
Cast off 4[5:6]sts at beg of next 2 rows. Cast off 2[3:4] sts at beg of next 2 rows. Dec 1 st at each end of next and every foll alt row 4 times in all. 78[84:90] sts. Work straight until armhole measures 7½[8:8¼]in 19[20:21]cm.
Shape shoulders
Cast off 7[8:9] sts at beg of next 2 rows. Cast off 6[7:8] sts at beg of next 4 rows. Cast off rem 40 sts.

Right Front
Using smaller needles and B work 7.5[8:8.5] points 75[80:85] sts.
Note: Half points worked for first and last sizes – work full points (as zigzag edging) first and end with half points. Continue as given for back to * and setting pattern 5 sts in from centre front edge – i.e. on RS rows knit 5 sts A, work 60 sts patt from chart, knit 10[15:20] sts A. Work in pattern as set throughout.
On 11th row dec 1 st at side edge of next and every foll 10th row 26 times, in all. 49[54:59] sts. Continue straight until front measures 36in (91cm) above points ending at centre front.

Shape neck

Dec 1 st at neck edge on next and every foll 4th row until front measures 40in (102cm) from top of points ending at armhole edge.

Shape armhole

Keeping neck dec correct as set, cast off 4[5:6]sts at armhole edge on next row, work 1 row. Cast off 2[3:4] sts at armhole edge on next row, work 1 row. Dec 1 st at armhole edge of next and every foll alt row 4 times in all. Cont to dec at neck edge until 19[22:25] sts rem. Work straight until armhole measures 7½[8:8½]in 19[20:21]cm ending at armhole edge.

Shape shoulder

Cast off 7[8:9] sts at beg of next row. Work 1 row. Cast off 6[7:8] sts at beg of next and foll alt row.

Left Front

Using smaller needles and B work 7.5[8:8.5] points. 75[80:85] sts.
Note: Half points worked for first and last sizes – work full points (as zigzag edging) first and end with half point. Work Complete as for right front but reversing all shaping.

Armhole band

Join shoulder seams.
With a 3.25mm circular needle and B, pick up and knit 90[100:110] sts evenly from armhole edge. Break the thread and leave these sts on the needle. Using B, work 9[10:11] points as given in zigzag edging and knit 1 (more) row. Holding the armhole RS facing you place the points needle behind it and cast off stitch by stitch from the two needles together. This gives a ridge on the RS which flattens when pressed.

Right front and neck edging

With a circular 3.25mm needle and B, beginning at the bottom edge of right front just above the points, pick up and knit the edge stitches to halfway across the back neck as follows:
190 sts to start of neck shaping, 65[70:75] sts to shoulder and 20 sts across half back neck. 275[280:285] sts. Make 27.5[28:28.5] points (positioning half points at centre back neck) and complete as given for armhole edging.

Left front and neck edging

Work as given for right front starting pick up at centre back neck and being sure to position half points for first and last sizes at centre back neck.

Finishing

Tidy loose ends back into their own colours. Block pieces to correct measurements. Join half points at centre back neck on first and last sizes. Join side seams. Press seams from inside. Make two twisted cords approx. 40½in (102cm) long. Attach cords approx. 7 zigzags down from shoulder seams.

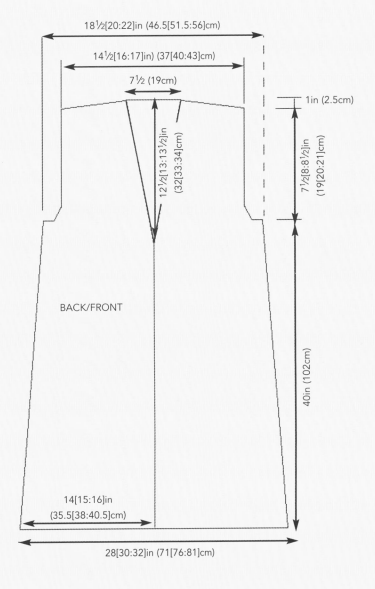

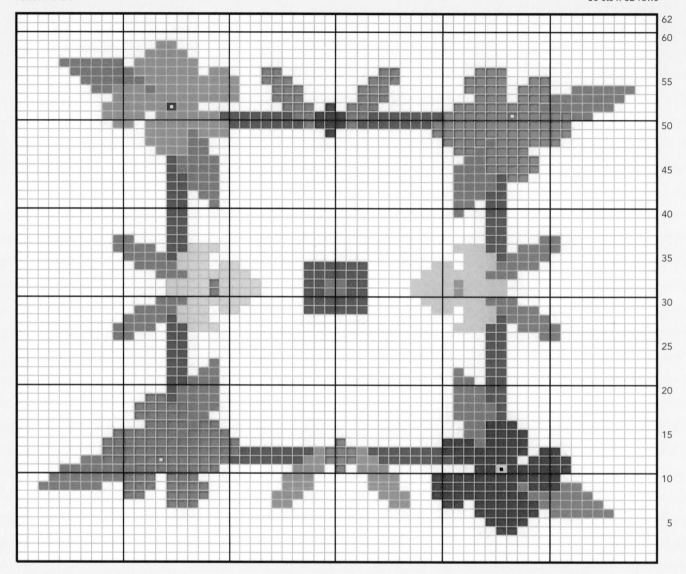

1 square = 1 st and 1 row
Read RS rows from R to L and
WS rows from L to R

Key

A B C D E F G H I

make bobble

Main image page 50

Baluchistan Stripe

A tribal woven rug from Baluchistan forms the basis of this relaxed summer jacket. Plaited embellishments are reminiscent of camel bags and travels taken through hot deserts.

SIZES
To fit bust 32[34:37:40:44]in (81[86:94:101:112]cm)
See schematic for actual measurements

MATERIALS
Rowan Summer Tweed 118yd (108m) per 50g hank
10[10:11:11:11] balls colour A: Raffia (515)
1[1:2:2:2] balls colour B: Reed (514)
1[1:1:1:1] balls colour C: Rush (507)
2[2:2:3:3] balls colour D: Sunset (509)
1[1:1:1:1] balls colour E: Toast (530)
2[2:2:2:2] balls colour F: Smoulder (522)
1[1:1:1:1] balls colour G: Choc Fudge (531)
Needles: 1 pair each 4.5mm (US 7) and 5mm (US 8), 4.5mm (US 7) circular needles
Stitch holder
Buttons: Approx. 40 x ½in (1.5cm)

TENSION
16 sts and 23 rows = 4in (10cm) measured over stocking stitch using larger needles.

STITCHES USED
Stocking stitch (page 144)
Garter stitch (page 144)
Eyelet holes (page 146)
2-colour stranded knitting (page 147)

Back
Using smaller needles and colour A cast on 88[92:96:100:104] sts.
Beg with a knit row, work in st st for 2 rows, ending with a WS row.
Row 3: (RS) K5(2:4:6:3), (yfwd, k2tog tbl, k3) 8[9:9:9:10] times, k1, (yfwd, k2tog tbl, k3) 7[8:8:8:9] times, yfwd, K2tog tbl, k5[2:4:6:3].
Beg with a purl row, work in st st for a further 3 rows, ending with a WS row.
Change to larger needles.
Using a combination of the **woven intarsia** technique (as described on page 148) and the **2-colour stranded knitting** technique (as described on page 147), and starting and ending rows as indicated, cont in patt from chart, until row 60 has been completed, ending with a WS row.
Break off all contrasts and cont in st st using colour A only.
Cont straight until back measures 26½[26¾:27:27½:28]in, (67[68:69:70:71]cm), ending with a WS row.

Shape shoulders and back neck
Cast off 10[11:11:12:12] sts at beg of next 2 rows. 68[70:74:76:80] sts.
Next row: (RS) Cast off 10[11:11:12:12] sts,
Knit until there are 15[14:16:15:17] sts on right needle and turn, leaving rem sts on a holder.
Work each side of neck separately.
Cast off 4 sts at beg of next row.
Cast off rem 11[10:12:11:13] sts.
With RS facing, rejoin yarn to rem sts, cast off centre 18[20:20:22:22] sts, knit to end.
Complete to match first side, reversing shapings.

Left Front
Using smaller needles and colour A cast on 45[47:49:51:53] sts
Beg with a knit row, work in st st for 2 rows, ending with a WS row.
Row 3: (RS) K5 [2:4:6:3], (yfwd, K2tog tbl, K3) 8[9:9:9:10] times.

Beg with a purl row, work in st st for a further 3 rows, ending with a WS row.
Change to larger needles.
Starting and ending rows as indicated, cont in patt from chart until chart row 60 has been completed, ending with a WS row.
Break off all contrasts and cont in st st using colour A only.
Cont straight until 38[38:38:40:40] rows less have been worked than on back to start of shoulder shaping, ending with a WS row.

Shape front slope
Dec 1 st at end of next and foll 10[12:12:13:13] alt rows, then on every foll 4th row until 31[32:34:35:37] sts rem.
Work 5 rows, ending with a WS row.

Shape shoulder
Cast off 10[11:11:12:12] sts at beg of next and foll alt row.
Work 1 row. Cast off rem 11[10:12:11:13] sts.

Right Front
Using smaller needles and colour A cast on 45[47:49:51:53] sts
Beg with a knit row, work in st st for 2 rows, ending with a WS row.
Row 3: (RS Eyelet row) (K3, yfwd, k2tog tbl) 8[9:9:9:10] times, k5 [2:4:6:3].
Complete to match left front, reversing shapings.

Sleeves
Using smaller needles and colour A cast on 42[42:44:46:46] sts
Beg with a K row, work in st st for 2 rows, ending with a WS row.
Row 3 (RS Eyelet row): K3 [3:4:5:5], (yfwd, k2tog tbl, k3) 7 times, yfwd, k2tog tbl, k2 [2:3:4:4].
Beg with a purl row, work in st st for a further 3 rows, ending with a WS row.
Change to larger needles.
Starting and ending rows as indicated, cont in patt from chart as folls:
Inc 1 st at each end of 3rd and every foll 4th row until there are 56[56:58:60:60] sts, taking inc sts into patt.
Work 1 row, ending with chart row 28 and a WS row.

Break off all contrasts and cont in st st using colour A only.
Inc 1 st at each end of 3rd and every foll 4th row to 74[74:78:74:86] sts, then on every foll 6th row until there are 80[80:84:84:88] sts.
Cont straight until sleeve measures 16[16:16½:16½:16½]in (41[41:42:42:42]cm), ending with a WS row.
Cast off.

Finishing

Tidy loose ends back into their own colours. Block pieces to correct measurements.
Join shoulder seams.

Front bands

Using circular needles and colour A and RSF pick up and knit one stitch for each row up R front, across back neck and down L front. Work 4 rows garter st. Cast off.
Using 4 strands of each colour, make plaits (see page 150) and attach as folls:
Using yarns D, F and G, make and attach plait across upper stripe in yarn B on each sleeve. In the same way, make and attach same colour plait to same stripe on back and fronts, extending this plait by 12in (30cm) at each front opening edge to form ties, tying knots at ends to form small tassels. Make and attach a plait across last stripe in C on back and fronts in same way but using yarns B, D and F, again extending this plait to form ties.

Using yarns B, D and F, make and attach plaits to run from neck, along shoulder seam and then down centre of sleeve, tying ends in a knot to form small tassel at cuff. Thread 2 strands each of yarns D and F and either yarn A, B or G through each eyelet hole of row 3 around lower edge of back and fronts, then plait these lengths to form a plait of 6in (15cm), tying ends in a knot to form a tassel. Using yarns A, D and F, make and attach plait to entire front opening and neck edge, extending ends 6in (15cm) below cast-on edge and tying knots to form small tassels.
Attach a button to row 3 of sleeves centrally between each eyelet hole. On body, attach buttons in same way but positioning buttons between every other eyelet hole.
Place centre of cast-off edge of sleeve to shoulder seam. Sew top of sleeve to body.
Join sleeve seams and side seams.
Steam seams.

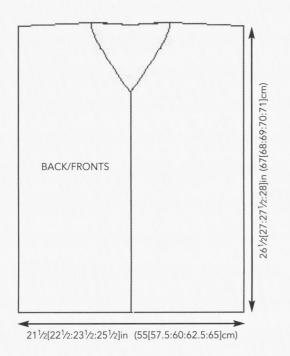

BACK/FRONTS

26½[27:27½:27½:28]in (67[68:69:70:71]cm)

21½[22½:23½:25½]in (55[57.5:60:62.5:65]cm)

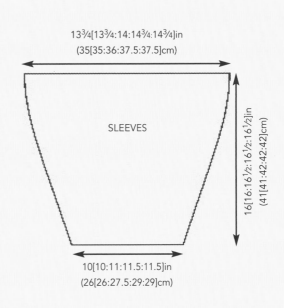

13¾[13¾:14:14¾:14¾]in (35[35:36:37.5:37.5]cm)

SLEEVES

16[16:16½:16½:16½]in (41[41:42:42:42]cm)

10[10:11:11.5:11.5]in (26[26:27.5:29:29]cm)

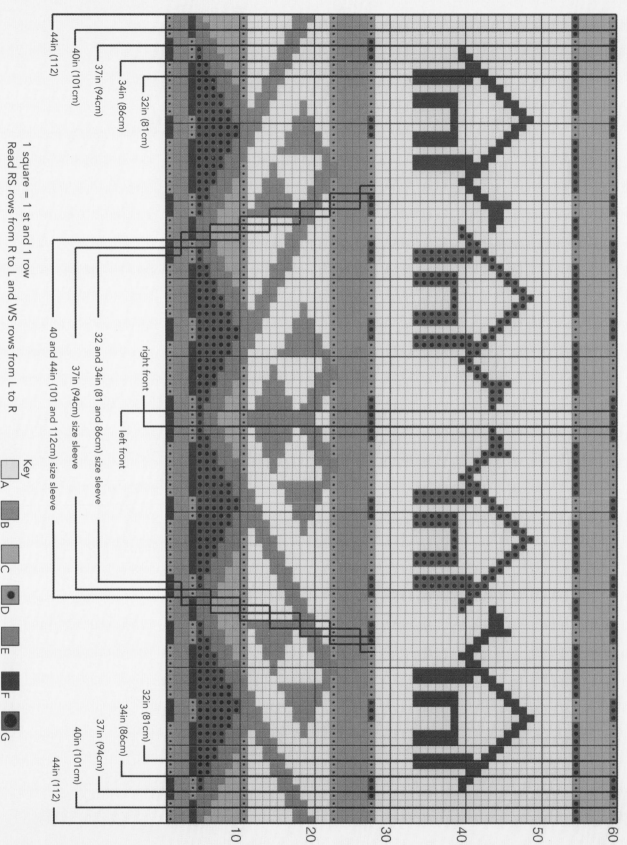

Pattern chart

44in (112)

40in (101cm)

37in (94cm)

34in (86cm)

32in (81cm)

1 square = 1 st and 1 row
Read RS rows from R to L and WS rows from L to R

right front

left front

32 and 34in (81 and 86cm) size sleeve

37in (94cm) size sleeve

40 and 44in (101 and 112cm) size sleeve

32in (81cm)

34in (86cm)

37in (94cm)

40in (101cm)

44in (112)

Key
A
B
C
D
E
F
G

10   20   30   40   50   60

Main image page 53

Suzani

Indian 'Suzanis' (embroidered hangings, or fabric coverings) were the inspiration for this relaxed and luxurious jacket. The ribbed shawl collar gives extra warmth for fireside relaxation.

SIZES

One size fits all 34–45½in (86–116cm)
See schematic for actual measurements

MATERIALS

UK Alpaca DK
290yd (265m) per 100g ball
8 balls colour A:
    Black
1 ball colour B:
    Mid-Green
1 ball colour C:
    Magenta
1 ball colour D:
    Dark Wine
1 ball colour E:
    Rose
1 ball colour F:
    Lilac
Needles: 1 pair each 3.75mm (US 5) and 4mm (US 6)

TENSION

21 sts and 31 rows = 4in (10cm) measured over st st intarsia pattern using larger needles.

STITCHES USED

2 x 2 rib (page 144)
Stocking stitch (page 144)

Back

Using larger needles and colour A cast on 150 sts and work 4 rows k2, p2 rib setting first row thus:
Row 1: (RS) *K2, p2, rep from * to last 2 sts, k2.
Start using a combination of the **woven intarsia** technique for the small flowers, and the **linked intarsia** technique for the large flowers (both described on page 148) and rep chart from bottom to top (row 1 to row 40) until back measures 32in (82cm).

Shape shoulders

Cast off 17 sts at beg of next 6 rows. Cast off rem 48 sts.

Left Front

Using larger needles and colour A cast on 75 sts and work 4 rows k2, p2 rib setting rib thus:
Row 1: (RS) *K2, p2, rep from * to last 3 sts, k3.
Row 2: K1, *p3, k2, rep from * to last 2 sts. p2.
Start and rep chart from bottom to top until work measures 18½in (47cm) from cast on edge.

Shape neck

Dec 1 st at neck edge on next and every foll 5th row until 51 sts rem. Work straight until front matches back to start of shoulder shaping.

Shape shoulder

Cast off 17 sts on next 3 alt rows.

Right Front

Work as for L front reversing shaping.

Sleeves

Using larger needles and colour A cast on 50 sts and work 6in (16cm) in k2, p2 rib. Follow chart from bottom to top, inc 1 st at both ends of next and every foll 3rd row until there are 110 sts, knitting extra sts in A only. Work straight until sleeve measures 21in (53cm).
Cast off.

Left Front Band and Collar

Using smaller needles and colour A cast on 20 sts.
Row 1: (RS) K3, (p2, k2) 4 times, k1.
Row 2: K1, (p2, k2) 4 times, p2.

These 2 rows form rib. Cont in rib until band, when slightly stretched, fits up L front opening edge to start of front slope shaping, ending with WS row.

Shape collar

Inc 1 st at beg of next and every foll alt row until 58 sts then every foll 4th row until there are 60 sts taking inc sts into rib. Cont straight until collar, (unstretched), fits up L front slope and across the centre back neck, ending with RS facing for next row. Cast off 8 sts at beg of next and foll 3 alt rows, then 7 sts at beg of foll 3 alt rows. Work 1 row. Cast off rem 7 sts.

Right Front Band and Collar

Work to match L front band and collar reversing shaping.

Belt

Using smaller needles and colour A cast on 20 sts. Work in k2, p2 rib, setting patt thus:
Row 1: (RS) K1, *k2, p2, rep from * to last 3 sts, K3.
Row 2: K1, *p2, k2, rep from * to last 3 sts, p2, k1.
Work until belt measures 55in (140cm). Cast off.

Finishing

Tidy loose ends back into their own colours. Block pieces to correct measurements, avoiding ribs.
Join shoulder seams, place markers 10in (25cm) down from shoulder seam at back and fronts. Sew on front bands and collar, then sew back seam of collar. Sew cast-off edge of sleeves to row ends above markers at back and fronts. Join sleeve and side seams. Steam seams.

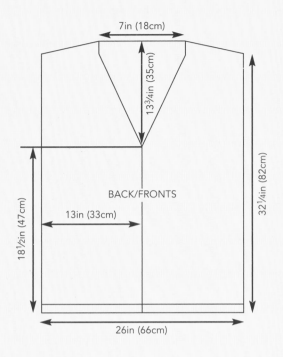

7in (18cm)

13¾in (35cm)

BACK/FRONTS

18½in (47cm)

13in (33cm)

32¼in (82cm)

26in (66cm)

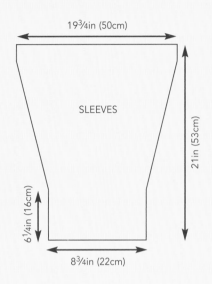

19¾in (50cm)

SLEEVES

21in (53cm)

6¼in (16cm)

8¾in (22cm)

Pattern chart

50 sts x 40 rows

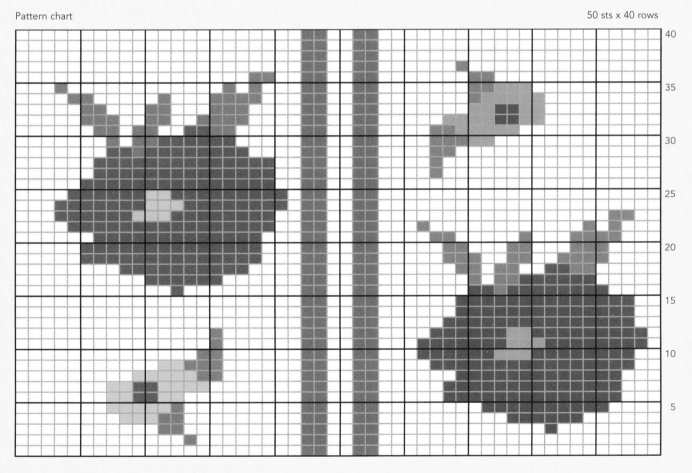

40

35

30

25

20

15

10

5

1 square = 1 st and 1 row
Read RS rows from R to L
and WS rows from L to R

Key

A   B   C   D   E   F   Use A and purl on a knit row, knit on a purl row

CHAPTER FIVE

Wraps & Scarves

Main image page 56

Columbine

Vertical lace and columbine motifs give this winter scarf all-round appeal – a fun twist is added with bright pompom embellishments.

SIZE
One size approx. 11in wide x 53in long (28 x 134.5cm), excluding pompoms.

MATERIALS
Rowan Scottish Tweed 4-ply 120yd (110m) per 25g ball
6 balls colour A:
    Midnight (23)
1 ball colour B:
    Sunset (11)
1 ball colour C:
    Machair (02)
1 ball colour D:
    Sea Green (06)
1 ball colour E:
    Brill Pink (10)
Rowan wool/cotton 123yd (113m) per 50g ball
1 ball Colour F: Bilberry (959)
Rowan RYC Cashsoft DK 142yd (130 m) per 50g ball
1 ball colour G:
    Poppy (512)
Needles: 1 pair each 2.75 mm (US 2) and 3.25 mm (US 4)
1½in (4cm) pompom maker

TENSION
26 sts and 38 rows to 4in (10cm) measured over pattern using larger needles.

STITCHES USED
Stocking stitch (page 144)
Moss (seed) stitch (page 144)
Pompom (page 151)

Little Vine Lace Pattern
Row 1: (RS) K4, yo, k1, k2tog.
Row 2: P2, p2tog tbl, p1, yo, p5.
Row 3: K6, yo, k1, k2tog, k1.
Row 4: P2tog tbl, p1, yo, p7.
Row 5: K3, k2tog, k1, yo, k4.
Row 6: P5, yo, p1, p2tog, p2.
Row 7: K1, k2tog, k1, yo, k6.
Row 8: P7, yo, p1, p2tog.
Repeat rows 1 – 8 throughout.

Scarf
With smaller needles and colour A cast on 82 sts.
Work 6 rows moss st (seed stitch).
Change to larger needles and, using the **woven intarsia** technique described on page 148, place pattern thus:
Work 6 sts in moss st), follow chart from st 1 to st 60 then work 10 sts in Little Vine pattern, then 6 sts in moss st (seed st).
Repeat chart from bottom to top 7 times (448 rows).
Next row: Moss st (seed stitch) 6, work in st st to last 6 sts. Moss st (seed stitch) 6.
Change to smaller needles and work 6 rows moss st (seed stitch). Cast off.

Finishing
Tidy loose ends back into their own colours.
Steam gently to correct measurements.
Make 4 pompoms in colour B, 4 with colour E and 2 with colour D.
Attach to ends of scarf using pic as guide.

53in (134.5cm)

11in (28cm)

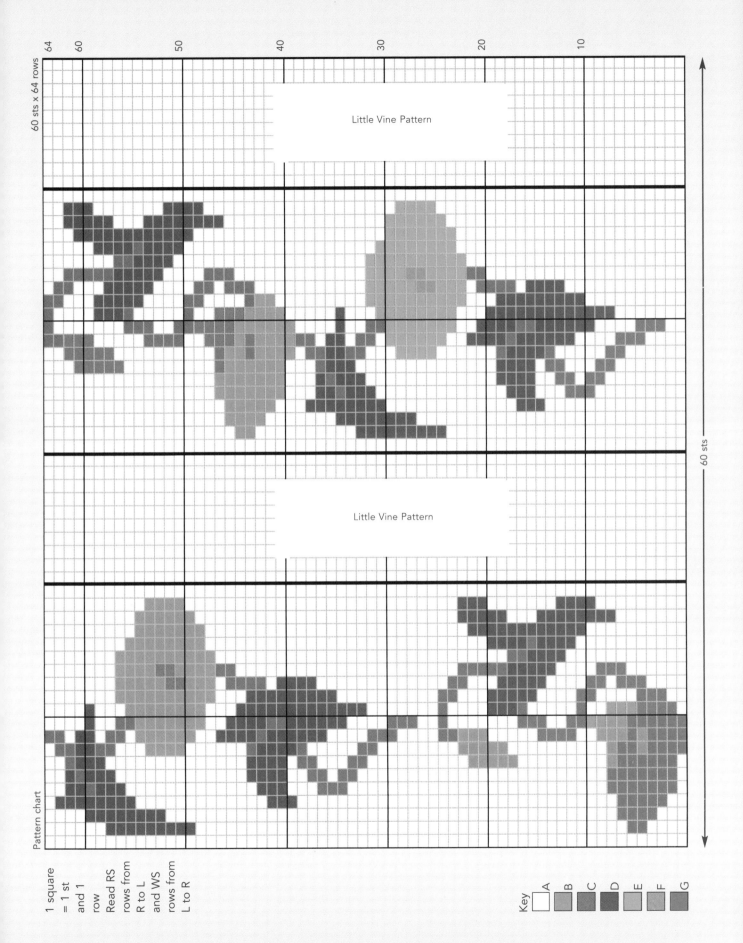

60 sts x 64 rows

64 60   50   40   30   20   10

Little Vine Pattern

Little Vine Pattern

60 sts

Pattern chart

1 square
= 1 st
and 1
row
Read RS
rows from
R to L
and WS
rows from
L to R

Key
A
B
C
D
E
F
G

Main image page 57

Laurel

Laurel leaves and berries dance across a background of moving colour. The crochet picot edge brings out the rust-coloured accents.

SIZES
One size: width 8in (22.5cm); length 75in (190cm)

MATERIALS
Rowan Tapestry
131yd (120m) per 50g ball
4 balls colour A:
    Moorland (175)
Rowan Felted Tweed
191yd (175m) per 50g ball
1 ball colour B:
    Treacle (145)
1 ball colour C:
    Bilberry (151)
1 ball colour D:
    Ginger (154)
Rowan Wool/Cotton
123yd (113m) per 50g ball
1 ball colour E:
    Shipshape (955)
1 ball colour F:
    Laurel (960)
1 ball colour G:
    Olive (907)
1 ball colour H:
    Rich (911)
Rowan Scottish Tweed DK
120yd (110m) per 50g ball
1 ball colour I:
    Claret (13)

Needles: 1 pair each 2.75 (US 2) and 3.25 (US 3)
1 x 2.25mm (US B1) crochet hook

TENSION
25sts and 35 rows = 4in (10cm) measured over st st and chart patt using larger needles.

STITCHES USED
Garter stitch (page 144)
Stocking stitch (page 144)
Crochet picot edge (page 153)

Scarf Panel (make 2)
Note: Scarf is made in 2 pieces and fabric is used sideways.
With smaller needles and colour E, cast on 240 sts. Work 4 rows in garter st. Change to larger needles and follow chart using the **woven intarsia** technique described on page 148, from bottom to top once, then rows 1–7 once more. Change to smaller needles and colour E and work 4 rows in garter st. Cast off.

Finishing
Tidy loose ends back into own their colours. Block pieces to correct measurements.
Sew scarf pieces tog along one side edge with cast on sides at bottom.
Side edge trims
With right side facing, smaller needles and colour E, pick up 74 sts along one side edge of scarf. Work 4 rows garter st. Cast off. Rep for other side edge of scarf.
Picot trim
With RS facing, colour D and crochet hook, work picot trim as foll: *ch3, sl st into same place (1 picot made), sl st 3; rep from * around 4 edges of scarf, sl st into first picot.
Steam seam.

75in (190cm)

8in (22.5cm)

Pattern chart

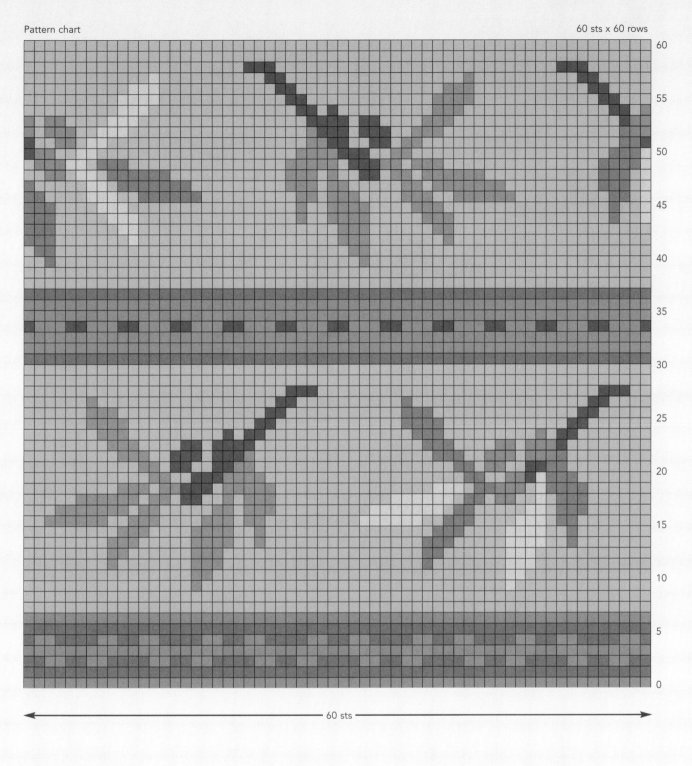

60

55

50

45

40

35

30

25

20

15

10

5

0

60 sts

1 square = 1 st and 1 row
Read RS rows from R to L and WS
rows from L to R

Key

A   B   C   D   E   F   G   H   I

Main image page 59

Lace Pashmina

Bands of triple leaf lace and autumnal geometrics join to make a long fringed Pashmina for autumn. This flexible piece can work in a myriad of ways making a useful addition to any wardrobe.

SIZES
One size 22in wide x 90in long (56 x 228.5cm) inc fringe

MATERIALS
Rowan Felted Tweed
191yd (175m) per 50g ball
7 balls main colour (MC):
    Treacle (145)
1 ball colour A:
    Ginger (154)
Rowan wool/cotton
123yd (113m) per 50g ball
1 ball colour B:
    Pumpkin (962)
1 ball colour C:
    Still (964)
Rowan Scottish Tweed DK
123yd (113m) per 50g ball
1 ball colour D:
    Lobster (17)
1 ball colour E:
    Sunset (11)
Needles: 1 pair each 3mm (US 3) and 3.75mm (US 5)

TENSION
22 sts and 24 rows = 4in (10cm) measured over st st and chart patt using larger needles.

STITCHES USED
Moss (seed) stitch (page 144)
Triple leaf lace (see right)
Stocking stitch (page 144)
Tassel (page 150)

Triple Leaf Lace
(Over 15 sts)
Note: sts are increased by 2 on row 5 and again on row 7, they are then decreased to the original number on rows 9 and 11.
Row 1: (RS) K1, yo, k2tog, k3tog, [yo, k1] 3 times, yo, k3tog tbl, ssk, yo, k1.
Row 2: and all WS rows Purl.
Row 3: K1, yo, k3tog, yo, k7, yo, k3tog tbl, yo, k1.
Row 5: K1, yo, k2tog, yo, k1, yo, k2, SK2P, k2, yo, k1, yo, ssk, yo, k1.
Row 7: K1, yo, k2tog, yo, k3, yo, k1, SK2P, k1, yo, k3, yo, ssk, yo, k1.
Row 9: K1, yo, [k2tog] twice, k3, yo, SK2P, yo, k3, [ssk] twice, yo, k1.
Row 11: K1, yo, [k2tog] 3 times, [k1, yo] twice, k1, [ssk] 3 times, yo, k1.
Row 12: Purl. Rep rows 1–12 for triple leaf lace patt .

Pashmina
With smaller needles and MC, cast on 115 sts. Work 7 rows in moss st. Purl 1 row on WS. Change to larger needles and, using the **woven intarsia** technique described on page 148, work in chart and lace patt, working 52 sts twice, then work first 11 sts once more, until piece measures 76in (193cm). Change to smaller needles and knit 1 row on RS. Work 7 rows moss st. cast off.

Finishing
Tidy loose ends back into their own colours.
Steam gently to correct measurements.
Attach 43 x 7in (110 x 18cm) fringe tassels to both ends of piece, matching colours of patts using picture as guide.

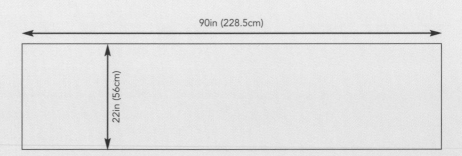

90in (228.5cm)

22in (56cm)

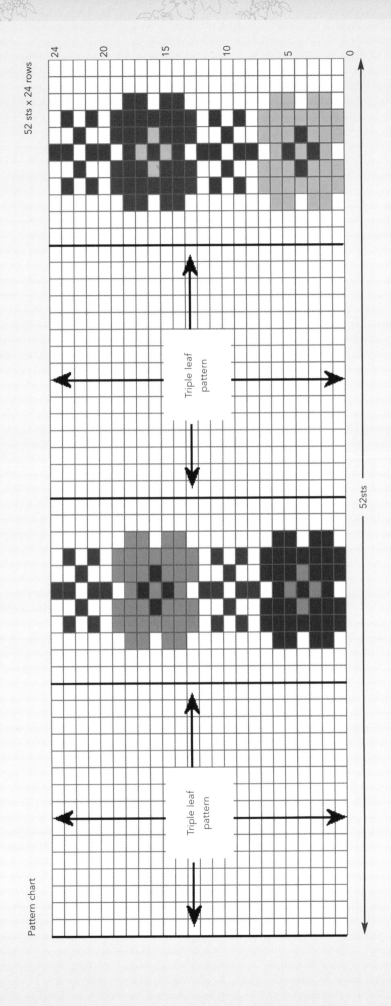

Pattern chart

52 sts x 24 rows

24
20
15
10
5
0

Triple leaf pattern

Triple leaf pattern

52sts

Key

MC

A
B
C
D
E

1 square = 1 st and 1 row
Read RS rows from R to L and WS
rows from L to R

CHAPTER SIX

Techniques

Basics

Reading patterns

In this book the smallest size –
usually 32in (81cm) – appears first,
followed by larger sizes in brackets.
Where only one figure is to be found
this figure relates to all sizes.

Needle sizes

METRIC	OLD UK	USA
2	14	0
2.25	13	1
2.5	—	—
2.75	12	2
3	11	—
3.25	10	3
3.5	—	4
3.75	9	5
4	8	6
4.5	7	7
5	6	8
5.5	5	9
6	4	10
6.5	3	10.5
7	2	10.5/11
7.5	1	10.5/11
8	0	11
9	00	13
10	000	15
12		17
15		19
20		35/36

Abbreviations

KNITTING

K (or k) — knit

P (or p) — purl

st(s) — stitch(es)

st st — stocking stitch (k1 row, p1 row, rep the 2 rows)

g-st — garter stitch (every row k)

sl — slip

ssk — slip, slip, knit (slip 2 consecutive sts then insert left needle back into the front of the 2 sts and k the two slipped sts together) – i.e. this forms a decrease

psso — pass slip stitch over

skpo — sl1, k1, pass slip st over the one just knitted

sk2p — sl1, k2tog, pass slip st over the k2tog

lp(s) — loop(s)

tbl — through back loop (i.e. ktbl or k tbl = k next st through back loop)

yf/yfwd — yarn forward (i.e. yarn to front)

yb — yarn back (i.e. yarn to back)

yo — yarn over needle to make a stitch (can mean yarn round needle to make a stitch)

k-wise — knit-wise (i.e as if to k st)

p-wise — purl-wise (i.e. as if to p st)

m1 — make 1 by picking up thread before next st and K into back of it

inc — increase

dec — decrease

k2tog — knit 2 together

p2tog — purl 2 together

beg — beginning

alt — alternate

foll — following

rnd — round

rep — repeat

patt — pattern

rem — remaining

cont — continue

cm — centimetre(s)

CN — cable needle

C4b — slip next 2 sts onto a CN and hold sts at back of the knitting, knit the next 2 sts and then the 2 sts rom the CN

C4f — slip next 2 sts onto a CN and hold sts at front of the knitting, knit the next 2 sts and then the 2 sts from the CN

L — left

R — right

RS — right side

WS — wrong side

RH — right hand

LH — left hand

RSF — right side facing

WSF — wrong side facing

CROCHET

ch — chain

dc — double crochet (US sc)

htr — half treble (US hdc)

tr — treble (US dc)

dtr — double treble (US tr)

sp — space

Basic Techniques

Cable cast-on

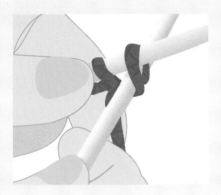

1

Make a slip knot approx 4in (10cm) from the yarn end. Hold the needle in left hand and place knot on needle. Insert right-hand needle through the front of the loop and under the left-hand needle, pass the working yarn under and over its tip. With right-hand needle draw the yarn through the slip knot to form a stitch. Transfer the new stitch to left-hand needle. Insert right-hand needle between 2 sts already made ready to make the next stitch.

2

Pass working yarn under and over tip of right-hand needle to make the next new stitch.

Continue in this way to cast on the required number of stitches.

Cable cast-off

1

Work first 2 sts in pattern, * insert tip of left-hand needle through the first stitch. Lift first stitch over second stitch and off the needle.

2

Work next st in pattern * Rep sequence from * to * until desired number of sts are cast off. Cut yarn and pull through last loop. Pull firmly to tighten loop.

1

2

Garter stitch

Knit every row.

Stocking stitch

Knit on right side rows and purl on wrong side rows. (Above) right side.

(Above) Stocking stitch, wrong side (reverse stocking stitch).

Moss stitch (seed stitch)

Row 1: *K1, p1; repeat from * to end
Row 2: Knit the purl sts and purl the knit sts.
Repeat row 2.

Twisted rib

1 x 1 twisted rib:
Even no of sts – **all rows**:
*K1b, p1 rep from * to end.
Odd no of sts –
Row 1: K1b, *p1, k1b rep from * to end.
Row 2: P1, *k1b, p1 rep from * to end.

2 x 2 twisted rib:
Even no of sts –
Row 1: *(k1b) twice, p2, rep from * to end.
Row 2: *k2, (p1b) twice, rep from * to end.
Repeat these 2 rows.

2 x 2 Rib

Row 1: *K2, p2, rep from *
Row 2: *p2, k2, rep from *
Repeat these 2 rows.

Cable 4 front (C4F)

1
Work to cable position, slip next 2 sts onto a cable needle and hold at front of work. Knit next 2 sts on the main needle.

2
Knit the 2 sts held on the cable needle.

Cable 4 back (C4B)

Work to cable position, slip next 2 sts onto a cable needle and hold at back of work.
Knit next 2 sts on the main needle.
Knit the 2 sts held on the cable needle.

Cable 8 front (C8F)

Work as for cable 4 front, slipping 4 sts onto cable needle and holding at front of work, knitting next 4 sts then knitting 4 sts held on cable needle.

Cable 8 back (C8B)

Work as for cable 4 back, slipping next 4 sts onto cable needle and holding at back of work, knitting next 4 sts, then knitting 4 sts held on cable needle.

Flower Centres

Bobbles can be knitted in different sizes, depending on how pronounced the centre of the flower needs to be. Here, two different designs illustrate a smaller bobble (Cable Flower, see also page 112) and a larger one which is formed by knitting three times into the same stitch (Caliope, see also page 122).

Bobbles can also be used to add texture to rib. Specific instructions or charts are given for rib and bobble placements used in these patterns.

Bobble (Cable Flower)

K into back and front of the stitch, turn. K2, turn, p2, turn, k2, turn. k2tog.

Bobble (Caliope)

Row 1: (K1, p1, k1) into next st, turn.
Row 2: K3, turn.
Row 3: P3, turn.
Row 4: K3tog.

1-row horizontal buttonhole

1

Work to buttonhole position, bring yarn to front and slip a stitch purl-wise. Place yarn at back * slip next stitch from left needle. Pass the first slipped stitch over it; rep from * three times more. Slip the last cast-off stitch to left needle and turn work.

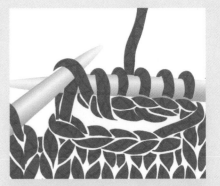

2

Using the cable cast-on with yarn at back, cast on 5 sts as follows: * Insert the right needle between the first and second stitches on the left-hand needle, draw up a loop, place the loop on the left-hand needle; rep from * four times more, turn work.

3

Slip the first stitch with yarn at the back from the left-hand needle and pass the extra cast-on stitch over it to close the buttonhole.

Eyelet holes

Simple eyelet holes for small buttons or decorative effects can be simply made by (yf, k2tog) – see Baluchistan Stripe, on page 126.

Knitting in Colour

Reading knitting charts

Each square on a knitting graph represents one stitch and each horizontal line of squares is a row of stitches. Charts are read from bottom to top. The knit rows (odd numbers) are read from right to left and the purl rows (even numbers) are read from left to right. Squares are coloured to indicate which yarn to use in each square. It can be useful to place a Post-it note or ruler one line above the row you are working on: this enables you to position the yarn ready for the next row.

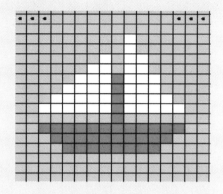

2 - colour stranded knitting

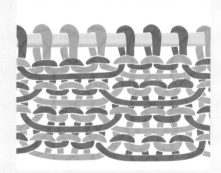

(*Above*) Two-colour stranded knitting, right side.

(*Above*) Two-colour stranded knitting, wrong side.

With this method of colour-knitting, one colour is held in the right hand and the second colour held in the left hand. Feed yarns into the stitches using chart as guide. Strand the yarn not in use loosely behind the stitches being worked. Do not strand over more than 3 stitches, catch yarn not in use by weaving under and over the main colour.

Intarsia (woven method)

(*Above*) Intarsia (woven method), right side.

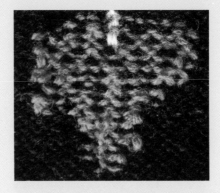

(*Above*) Intarsia (woven method), wrong side.

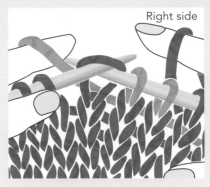

Right side

Right side

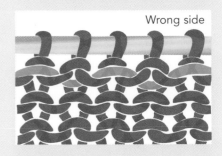

Wrong side

This method is similar to two-colour stranded knitting. The main colour (the one that shows on the front) is held in the right hand and the 'carry' colour (the one that will be woven behind the main colour) is held in the left hand. The carried yarn is brought alternately above and below each stitch made, so that it is woven in as you go.

Use small balls or bobbins of yarn for the motif colours and weave background yarn along behind motifs.

This makes a firm double thickness fabric where the motifs occur giving a slightly 3D effect.

Intarsia (linked method)

(*Above*) Right side of intarsia.

(*Above*) Wrong side of intarsia.

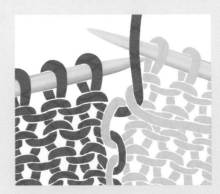

I use this method very occasionally where a large motif forms part of the design and it is too far to 'weave in' the background colour from one side to the other. Link the two colours around each other, pulling firmly to avoid holes.

Finishing your Garments

Bands (sewn on)

After blocking the main pieces of the garment to the correct measurements with right side facing, pin the band at the top and bottom. Ease the band gently to stretch across required length, pin at 2in (5cm) intervals. Slip stitch band into position.

(Above) Right side.

(Above) Wrong side.

Picking up and knitting edge stitches

(Above) Stitches picked up to knit into a button band (wrong side).

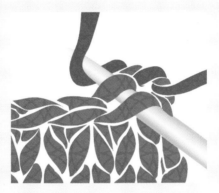

With right-side facing, insert needle under cast off loops in the row below the cast-off edge, or one stitch in from side edge if picking up front bands.

With right-hand needle knit-wise *(above left)* draw the yarn through to make a stitch *(above right)*.

Bands (picked up)

Bands can be picked up both horizontally (e.g. neckbands), vertically (e.g. front bands) and diagonally (e.g. Pebble, page 84). In all cases pick up 1 st for each st or row using a needle 2 sizes smaller than the needle used for main body of work (e.g. body knitted on 3mm [US 4] needles, band picked up and knitted on 2mm [US 2] needles).

(Above) Right side.

(Above) Wrong side.

Sewing up/mattress (US Kitchener) stitch

This method of sewing up is ideal for colour-patterned knitwear as it is done with right side facing and motifs can be matched up as you go. It provides a strong and invisible seam.

Place the two seam edges side by side. *Insert threaded needle through two stitch bars one stitch in from the edge on one side, then pick up the two stitch bars one stitch in on the opposite side*, without pulling the stitches taut. Rep from * to * two or three times more. Pull thread taut and seam will glide together. Repeat instructions until seam is complete.

(*Above*) Right side.

(*Above*) Wrong side.

Fringe tassels

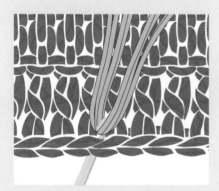

Wrap yarn around a cardboard rectangle slightly deeper than required length of fringe. Cut along one edge to make strands. Fold fringe lengths in half.

With crochet hook pull fold through edge of knitting.

Bring ends back through loop, pull down to neaten and secure.

Plaited tassels

Work as for fringe tassels, making 2 or 3 strands of each of 3 colours. When tassel is secured, plait to required length and knot end to secure. Trim ends.

Twisted cord

Cut lengths of yarn three times the desired finished length. Knot ends. Place one end over a finger, hook or door knob (1) and twist strands clockwise until they try to turn back on themselves. Keeping strands tightly stretched, fold pieces in half and let go of one end. Allow cord to twist onto itself. Knot ends to secure (2).

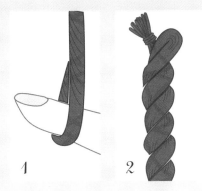

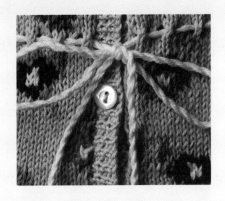

Pompoms

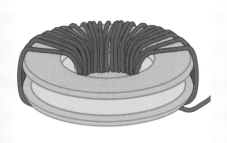

1
Cut two cardboard circles to desired size of finished pompom. Cut a hole one third of total diameter in the centre. Wrap yarn around cardboard circles as shown above.

2
Continue wrapping until central hole is full. Cut through yarn at outer edge, between cardboard circles.

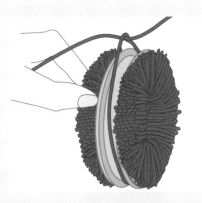

3
Ease circles apart and wrap a length of yarn tightly round central strands. Knot tightly. Pull off cardboard circles. Fluff out pompom and trim. Use dangling threads to attach to knitting.

Basic Crochet Techniques

Crochet chain

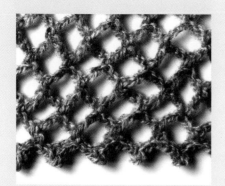

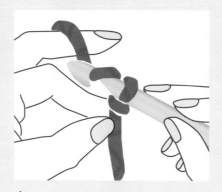

1

Make a slip knot, yarn over hook.

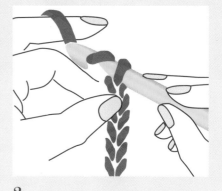

2

Draw the yarn through to form a new loop.

Continue until required number of chains have been made.

Crochet slip stitch

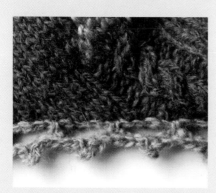

Insert hook into the work, yarn over and draw the yarn through both the work and loop on the hook in one movement.

Double crochet (US single crochet)

1
Join in yarn. Insert hook under next two bars of cast-on or cast-off edge. Wrap yarn over hook and draw yarn through work

2
Wrap yarn again and draw yarn through both loops on hook.

Treble crochet (US double crochet)

1
Yarn over hook, insert hook into work (4th ch from hook) yarn over hook, draw though work only and yarn over hook again.

2
Yarn round hook draw through last 2 loops on hook.

Crochet picot edge

Working into sts of cast-on or cast-off edge: 1 dc into first stitch, * 4ch, 1 dc into same place as last dc **
1 dc into each of next 2 sts, rep from * to end, ending last rep at **.

Resources

Distributors of Rowan and Jaeger yarns

AUSTRALIA
Australian Country Spinners, 314
Albert Street, Brunswick,
Victoria 3056
Tel: +61 3 9380 3888
Fax: +61 3 9387 2674
E-mail: sales@auspinners.com.au

AUSTRIA
Coats Harlander GmbH,
Autokaderstrasse 31, A -1210 Wien.
Tel: +43 01 27716 – 0
Fax: +43 01 27716 – 228

BELGIUM
Pavan, Meerlaanstraat 73, B9860
Balegem (Oosterzele)
Tel: +32 9 221 8594
Fax: +32 9 221 8594
E-mail: pavan@pandora.be

CANADA
Diamond Yarn, 9697 St Laurent,
Montreal, Quebec, H3L 2N1
Tel: +1 514 388 6188

Diamond Yarn (Toronto),
155 Martin Ross, Unit 3, Toronto,
Ontario, M3J 2L9
Tel: +1 416 736 6111
Fax: +1 416 736 6112
E-mail: diamond@diamondyarn.com
Web: www.diamondyarn.com

DENMARK
Coats Danmark A/S,
Marienlunds Allé 4, 7430 Ikast
Tel: +45 96 60 34 00
Fax: +45 96 60 34 08
E-mail: coats@coats.dk

FINLAND
Coats Opti Oy, Ketjutie 3,
04220 Kerava
Tel: +358 9 274 871
Fax: +358 9 2748 7330
E-mail: coatsopti.sales@coats.com

FRANCE
Coats France/Steiner Frères, 100,
avenue du Général de Gaulle, 18 500
Mehun-Sur-Yèvre
Tel: +33 02 48 23 12 30
Fax: +33 02 48 23 12 40

GERMANY
Coats GMbH, Kaiserstrasse 1,
D-79341 Kenzingen
Tel: +49 7644 8020
Fax: +49 7644 802399
Web: www.coatsgmbh.de

HOLLAND
de Afstap, Oude Leliestraat 12, 1015
AW Amsterdam
Tel: +31 20 6231445
Fax: +31 20 427 8522

HONG KONG
East Unity Co Ltd, Unit B2,
7/F Block B, Kailey Industrial Centre,
12 Fung Yip Street, Chai Wan
Tel: +852 2869 7110
Fax: +852 2537 6952
E-mail: eastuni@netvigator.com

ICELAND
Storkurinn, Laugavegi 59, 101
Reykjavik
Tel: +354 551 8258
E-mail: malin@mmedia.is

ITALY
D.L. srl, Via Piave, 24 – 26, 20016
Pero, Milan
Tel: +39 02 339 10 180
Fax: +39 02 33914661

JAPAN
Puppy-Jardin Co Ltd, 3-8-11
Kudanminami Chiyodaku,
Hiei Kudan Bldg. 5F, Tokyo
Tel: +81 3 3222-7076
Fax: +81 3 3222-7066
E-mail: info@rowan-jaeger.com

KOREA
Coats Korea Co Ltd, 5F Kuckdong
B/D, 935-40 Bangbae- Dong,
Seocho-Gu, Seoul
Tel: +82 2 521 626.
Fax: +82 2 521 5181

LEBANON
y.knot, Saifi Village, Mkhalissiya
Street 162, Beirut
Tel: +961 1 992211
Fax: +961 1 315553
E-mail: HYPERLINK
"mailto:y.knot@cyberia.net.lb"
y.knot@cyberia.net.lb

NEW ZEALAND
Please contact Rowan for details
of stockists

NORWAY
Coats Knappehuset AS, Pb 100 Ulste,
5873 Bergen
Tel: +47 55 53 93 00
Fax: +47 55 53 93 93

SINGAPORE
Golden Dragon Store, 101 Upper
Cross Street #02-51, People's Park
Centre, Singapore 058357
Tel: +65 6 5358454
Fax: +65 6 2216278
E-mail: gdscraft@hotmail.com

SOUTH AFRICA
Arthur Bales PTY, PO Box 44644,
Linden 2104
Tel: +27 11 888 2401
Fax: +27 11 782 6137

SPAIN
Oyambre, Pau Claris 145, 80009
Barcelona
Tel: +34 670 011957
Fax: +34 93 4872672
E-mail: oyambre@oyambreonline.com

SWEDEN
Coats Expotex AB, Division Craft,
Box 297, 401 24 Goteborg
Tel: +46 33 720 79 00
Fax: +46 31 47 16 50

SWITZERLAND
Coats Stroppel AG, CH -5300 Turgi (AG)
Tel: +41 562981220
Fax: +41 56 298 12 50

TAIWAN
Laiter Wool Knitting Co Ltd, 10-1 313
Lane, Sec 3, Chung Ching North
Road, Taipei
Tel: +886 2 2596 0269
Fax: +886 2 2598 0619

USA
Westminster Fibers Inc, 4 Townsend
West, Suite 8, Nashua,
New Hampshire 03063
Tel: +1 603 886 5041/5043
Fax: +1 603 886 1056
E-mail: rowan@westminsterfibers.com

UK
Rowan, Green Lane Mill, Holmfirth,
West Yorkshire, England HD9 2DX
Tel: +44 (0) 1484 681881
Fax: +44 (0) 1484 687920
E-mail: mail@knitrowan.com
Web: www.knitrowan.com

**For stockists in all other countries
please contact Rowan for details.**

Distributors of other yarns

UK ALPACA
Vulscombe Farm, Cruwys Morchard,
Tiverton, Devon EX16 8NB
Tel: +44 (0) 01884 243 579
Fax: +44 (0) 01884 243 514
E-mail: info@ukalpaca.com
Web: www.ukalpaca.com

BROWN SHEEP COMPANY
1 00 662 County Road 16, Mitchell,
Nebraska 69357, USA
Tel: +1 308 635 2198
E-mail: pwells@brownsheep.com
Web: www.brownsheep.com

DALE OF NORWAY
5721 Dalekvam, Norway
Tel: +47 56 59 54 00
Fax: +47 56 59 54 50
E-mail: daleofnorway@dale.no
Web: www.dale.no

DALE OF NORWAY – USA
Distributor: Inc. 4750 Shelburne
Road, Suite 20, SHELBURNE, VT
05482 USA
Tel: +1 802 383 0132
Fax: +1 802 383 0133
E-mail: mail@daleofnorway.com

JAMIESON AND SMITH
90 North Road, Lerwick, Shetland
ZE1 0PQ, UK
Tel: +44 (0) 1595 693 579
Fax: +44 (0) 1595 695 009
E-mail: sales@shetlandwool.org
Web: www.shetlandwoolbrokers.co.uk

Acknowledgements

Photography
Chris Gloag

Stylist
Jane Postlethwaite

Models
Willow Boswell-Wright
Bailee Roupe at MOT

Shoes and clothing
Yoma
www.yomauk.com

Organic clothing
Jaba Yard
www.jabayard.com

Pattern checking
Carol Chambers

Technique photography
GMC Publications

Author's Acknowledgements

I have the following fabulous editors to thank for commissioning this collection of knitwear designs: Kate Taylor, former editor of *Knitting* magazine, Kate Buller from *Rowan*, Trisha Malcolm, Editorial Director, *Vogue Knitting* magazine, and Kandy Regis from *Woman's Weekly*. Although each magazine has a different look and style, my classic designs fit in well with each individual editor's concepts of quality timeless knitwear.

Thank you to Gerrie Purcell of GMC Publications for helping me put this group of patterns into a book, to Carol Chambers for tirelessly checking patterns, graphs and techniques, Gill Parris for keeping me on track, Gilda Pacitti for managing the art direction and James Hollywell for the design. GMC are a great team to work with.

Special thanks go to my dedicated knitters: Chris Bebbington, Mary Coe, Yvonne Fairall, Glennis Garnett, Bernice Ingram, Elaine Longbottom, Linda Robertson, Shirley Taylor, Ruth White and Ann Wren, without whose fantastic professional skills there would be no garments.

Thank you to Rowan, Jaeger, Jamison & Smith, UK Alpaca, Brown Sheep and Dale of Norway for letting me play with their innovative yarns.

Thank you to my good friend and secretary Beryl Smith who helps me ride the twists and turns of the textile world with an unfailing sense of humour.

Last, but not least, thank you to all my fans who knit and wear my designs. Your continued enthusiasm and support keeps me on my creative path.

Author's contact details

Sasha Kagan
The Studio
Y-Fron
Llawr-y-Glyn
Caersws
Powys
SY17 5RJ
UK
E-mail: sasha@sashakagan.co.uk
Web: www.sashakagan.co.uk

Custom-made garments and knitting kits are available to order. Please send to the address above for prices.

Other books by Sasha Kagan

Crochet Inspiration
Sixth & Spring Books, 2007
UK Distributor GMC Publications
ISBN 1-933027-12-6

Knitting for Beginners
Carroll & Brown, 2004
ISBN 1 903258-90-1
USA: **Ready Set Knit**
Creative Publishing International
ISBN 13978-1-58923-185-6

Sasha Kagan's Country Inspiration
The Taunton Press, 2000
ISBN 1-56158-338-3

Sasha Kagan's Big and Little Sweaters
Dorling Kindersley, 1987
ISBN 0-86318-248-8

The Sasha Kagan Sweater Book
Dorling Kindersley, 1984
ISBN 0-86318- 051-5

Signed copies of all Sasha's books are available from her studio.

Index

Page numbers in *italics* refer to photographs of projects.

To place an order, or to request a catalogue,
please contact:

GMC Publications Ltd, Castle Place,
166 High Street, Lewes, East Sussex
BN7 1XU, United Kingdom
Tel: 01273 488005
Fax: 01273 402866
www.gmcbooks.com

Orders by credit card are accepted